PURCHASING MANAGEMENT IN THE SMALLER COMPANY

Floyd D. Hedrick

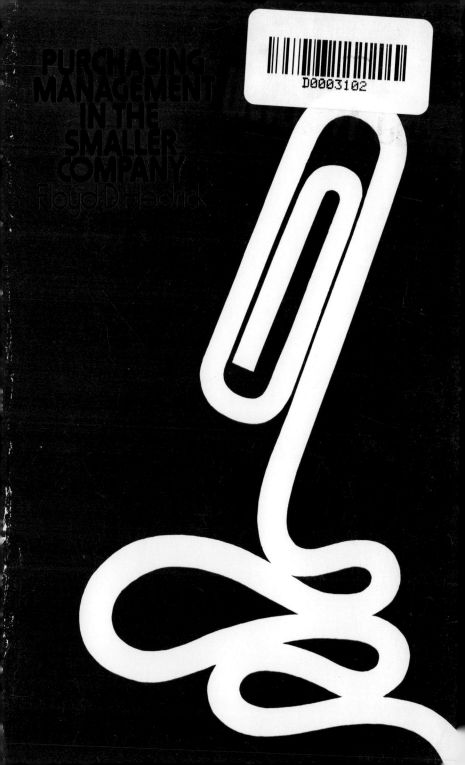

Purchasing Management
in the Smaller Company

Purchasing Management in the Smaller Company

Floyd D. Hedrick

American Management Association, Inc.

International standard book number: 0–8144–2147–4
Library of Congress catalog card number: 72–141681

To

Rachel, Susan, and Alice
for their patience and understanding

I gratefully acknowledge the enthusiastic and untiring
efforts of my secretary, Mrs. Nena Chamberlin, who typed
the manuscript for this book in her off-duty hours. In addition, I acknowledge my deep appreciation for the encour-
agement and support of my colleagues at The Macke
Company.

Contents

THE NEWLY APPOINTED PURCHASING MANAGER

Congratulations! You have just been appointed purchasing manager of your company. You will no doubt contemplate the many facets of your new position and ask yourself: "What do I do now that I haven't done before?" In this book we shall analyze the job of the purchasing manager of a small company and, in doing so, perhaps help you accomplish a better job for your company.

When you, as a former buyer for example, become a purchasing manager, you assume a position of greater responsibility in the company, and the usual personnel department formalities of showing you around the office are not enough to insure proper orientation. Your superiors should ease the transition with an in-depth orientation. This orientation is primarily the job of two men—the line official who had the final voice in selecting you as the new manager and the official to whom you will report.

The orientation should encompass three broad areas. First is the big picture, which outlines the company's objectives and future plans. You should make a point of understanding the attitudes of top management. Second is the operation picture, or setting, in which you will operate. This should be a rundown of areas of coordination, interdepartmental relations, and your area of responsibility. Finally, you should have a heart-to-heart talk with the official who selected you and your new boss on how to avoid pitfalls in the company and how to continue advancing. After all this preparation there is still much you will have to discover for yourself, but this probing and stock-taking must nevertheless be done.

The kind of responsibilities you accept and the way you carry them out will tell what kind of purchasing manager and leader you are. Let us now identify a purchasing manager, from both a purchasing and a managing viewpoint. On the purchasing side there are several key jobs. You must establish purchasing goals and objectives, and follow through on them; negotiate contracts for individual high dollar value materials and for groups of materials; communicate clearly—with your own purchasing department personnel, with other departments, and with top management; keep a close relationship with suppliers; and visit suppliers' plants on a regular basis.

On the managing side there are five key characteristics of a good manager: drive, intellectual ability, leadership, organizing ability, and initiative. Perhaps we should add one other important asset of a good manager—the art of listening. Managers must listen objectively, sensitively, and sincerely. In manager-subordinate meetings, do not assume that you and your subordinate will reach the same conclusion from a specific set of facts. Evaluate what's being said. Is he saying only what he thinks you want to hear? Is he holding back to avoid sounding disloyal? Pay attention to physical cues such as smiles, grimaces, scowls, or silences; these can be as important as words. Accept ideas without condescension. Be objective. Maintain a receptive attitude, no matter how bad the news or how hostile the critic. Unless you listen to what your subordinate wants you to know for his benefit, he won't tell you what you want to know for your benefit. Do not let your own position be known first, or you will not receive a truly free opinion.

To perform effectively as part of the management team, a purchasing manager must develop three basic traits that are essential to management: insight, foresight, and hindsight.

These characteristics are even more important in purchasing than in other branches of management. A concern with prices, quality, and service is only part of the job. Now that purchasing is receiving increasing recognition as an actual management function, the purchasing manager must operate in very human terms.

You are involved daily in the demanding business of dealing with people—from salesmen to people involved in every aspect of your company's operations. This is where the need for insight enters the picture—the insight of human experience. In many instances it is the purchasing manager who first represents his company to the visitor or the salesman who hopes to receive his business and his trust. In this sense you must be a psychologist as well as a purchaser of materials and services; you must exercise judgment, not only of materials but of men. You also have to be a salesman to get that little "extra" that involves service and slight advantage over the competition.

Where does foresight come into the picture? A purchasing manager is a specialist charged with the responsibility for spending roughly half his company's sales income each year. You must have the ability to anticipate trends, needs, and shifts in the marketplace, as well as within your own organization. This, of course, is a vital function of management at every level—the recognition of subtle changes that could prove to be significant a few months or years from now.

Hindsight too is vital to the purchasing manager's responsibilities. In this context, we define hindsight as the capacity to learn from experience, and never stop learning. It's the knowledge that you should take nothing for granted, no matter how many times it seemingly has been proved before.

These are essential components of truly creative management, and nowhere are they more important than in the purchasing function. In today's complex business climate, one branch of management leans heavily on all the others, and if there were no sound purchasing policy, other managers would lack the tools and means to produce goods for the marketplace.

TIME ALLOCATION

Do you have the time to be a good purchasing manager? Everyone wishes he had more time to get his work done, and this is especially true of the purchasing manager of a small company. There simply never seems to be enough time. The secret is to salvage minutes. The busiest people in the world are minute snatchers, and they accomplish a great deal in these saved minutes. There are 1,440 minutes in a day and you say, "Yes, but I use only 480 of those precious minutes on my job." If you are a purchasing manager of any size company, it simply isn't so if you're doing an effective job.

Before proceeding, I think it apropos to quote Victor Hugo.

> He who every morning plans the transactions of the day, and follows that plan, carries a thread that will guide him through the labyrinth of the most busy life. The orderly arrangement of his time is like a ray of light which darts itself through all his occupations. But, where no plan is laid, where the disposal of time is surrendered merely to the chance of incidents, all things lie huddled together in one chaos, which admits of neither distribution nor review.*

Whether you are purchasing manager of a small department or of a multiplant operation, lack of time is a common gripe. It is certainly true that the purchasing manager today is in a constant race with time, but what can we do about it?

DAILY PLANNING

Perhaps one of our problems is that we, like other human beings, tend to cling to the known and familiar routine. The fact that we may hold the title of purchasing manager—an

* As quoted by Raymond Schuessler in "The Fine Art of Saving Time," *The Sample Case* (United Commercial Travelers of America, Feb. 1967), p. 11.

executive position—and sit in a high place in our company doesn't automatically endow us with a sense of order, discipline, and consistency. In short, as far as the allocation of time is concerned we can be as dumb as the next fellow and, as a consequence, work harder at our job than necessary. For example, as purchasing manager you might be particularly vulnerable to wasting time by stretching your lunch period. In addition, the routine of purchasing is likely to stifle initiative, creativity, and planning follow-through. Your daily concerns tend to keep you almost continuously involved with exacting but all too familiar detail—with such items as commodity data, price trends, forms and procedures, buying techniques, interviewing salesmen, and the myriad mechanical motions and formularized follow-through that must be done with complete accuracy to insure that no dollar is lost, no hour is wasted, no man, machine, or tool is down for lack of one or another ingredient, part, or action needed to maintain production at specified levels.

Even so, as purchasing manager you must find the time, somehow, to do intelligent thinking and planning on your own. A portion of the crowded day must be set aside and made inviolate against invasion or interruption. Many purchasing managers waste time in their dealings with others, especially in long drawn-out conversations. Much time is demanded by requisitioners and suppliers; thus interviewing techniques must be tightened up to keep the discussion on matters of business. Before attending a meeting or conference, you should spend some time organizing your thoughts. Talking about useless matters becomes a habit, and soon you will find yourself giving sermons instead of short declarations of need and intent. You must also be careful about relations with your purchasing personnel. Beware of close supervision or overdirection of personnel involved in routine buying activities. An effective purchasing manager understands the advantage of leaving personnel on their own to figure out a few details. Furthermore, repeated demands of proof of progress merely interferes with performance.

Once you have identified the problems that are costing you valuable time and have taken concrete steps to solve them, you can zero in on other areas such as those daily activities where control of time spent is largely in your own hands. A good rule to begin with is to delegate every task that doesn't require your personal attention. As we said before, if you cling to routine matters, you will never get out from under the clerical burden. Perhaps your secretary or a clerk can handle many of these routine duties. Even if you don't have an assistant, you can establish other methods. For example, you could let your using departments write their own releases against blanket purchase orders. Many small firms ask supplier salesmen to handle much of the paperwork involved in listing requirements, pricing various items, and maintaining catalogs in order. Another time saver that might be considered for both internal and external communications is simply to use a form letter or other printed notice to get your message across. This is always faster and less costly than writing a formal letter, making a long-distance call, or setting up a meeting with a salesman.

As part of your campaign to save time, you should plan ahead, anticipate time-consuming projects, and make every effort to stagger the dates of projects. Blanket purchase order expiration dates should be staggered so that just a few agreements come up for renegotiation periodically throughout the year. If your company has a slack season, save this time for plant visits and complex negotiations. In addition, just as you combine several requisitions on one purchase order, you can, in many instances, combine daily activities. This means making the maximum use of every interview by discussing all important matters still unresolved between you and the salesman or department head.

The effective purchasing manager will, of necessity, be somewhat aggressive in the management of his time. You cannot afford to be a "nice guy" to each and every person in your company or even to outsiders. For example, personal purchases should be discouraged, and you should insist that requisitions be complete before forwarding to purchasing. If a requisition is received that is not clear, return it to the originator for clarification. There are two essentials to remember about time. First, it is not elastic; no matter how much you need, the supply is always limited to the hours in a day. Second, it is irreplaceable; once gone it cannot be recovered.

One way to increase productivity is to make up a daily list of "must do" projects. You need not have a fancy form, a simple legal pad will do. At the end of each day jot down the projects you plan to do the next day and rank them in order of importance. You may wish to have a second page for a list of future must-do projects. If you adopt this simple system, you will enjoy the benefits almost immediately. To name a few: You will know which of the day's problems require immediate attention, and the order of their importance; you will have a record of your daily activities in one place rather than in various memos and desk drawers; omission of an essential project will not be the frequent problem it was before you began this habit; essential things will be done; and your chaotic days will gradually assume a marvelous, yet flexible, order.

ADVANCE PLANNING

We have discussed the daily allocation of time. What about advance planning? Many purchasing managers let themselves get so involved in current problems and crises that they rarely get a chance to spend enough time on advance planning of their activities. The effective purchasing manager must plan for the future. The more crowded and hectic your schedule, the more important it is that you take the time to do some advance thinking.

You must get a feel for what lies in store for next week, next month, next year, and, yes, even five years ahead. What big projects do you see coming down the pike? How far ahead must you issue the purchase orders for on-time delivery? Do you anticipate other problems and obstacles? Wouldn't it be a good idea to draw up a timetable and get ahead of your problems by figuring out what should be done now to insure smooth sailing later? Once you've evolved a plan, don't keep it to yourself. Discuss your intentions with your key personnel and listen to their suggestions; even the best of plans can be improved. Your plans will be stronger, not weaker because of it.

Another way to save time for more essential work is to review all your procedures periodically and simplify your work when feasible. You must do this if you are to keep your head above water. The effective purchasing manager will take the time to think about simplifying not only his own job, but the jobs of others in his department. The employees in your department need your guidance in deciding what's important, what can be dispensed with, and how to get the best results with the least effort. When reviewing your own job and those of others, you may discover that some methods or procedures have been altered unwisely or without proper authorization. In other words, people aren't doing what they're supposed to be doing.

Your job as purchasing manager demands that you never become too busy to plan in advance. The purchasing manager who makes his plans in advance is making an intelligent effort to dictate the future. The purchasing manager who doesn't will find the future dictating to him.

MANAGEMENT BY OBJECTIVES

No doubt you have heard the slogan "management by objectives" bantered around in conversations on management. If ten different people are asked to define management by objectives, you usually get ten different answers—all with some validity.

In The Macke Company, when we say that our company has a management-by-objectives program, we mean that each level of management, from the presidential level down, establishes specific goals or targets it expects to achieve monthly, quarterly, and yearly. At the end of each period, the actual results achieved are measured against the original goals. The purchasing manager, for example, may establish a goal of achieving certain reductions in cost of goods, of reducing the number of suppliers by consolidating volume, or of improving purchasing procedures.

In structuring for management by objectives, it is necessary to start at the top and define the function of the president and the company's objectives. The sum of the objectives of all other functions under the president should equal the total objectives of the company. It is vitally important, therefore, to have excellent communications among all levels of management for the purpose of effecting the interdepartmental team effort necessary to achieve company objectives. Furthermore, top-level managers must recognize the psychological factors inherent in the system and make strong efforts to bring the lower-level managers together to explain to each other what their plans are. In other words, each manager must clearly identify the objectives he wishes to achieve and set a date by which he expects to achieve them. One of the biggest pitfalls in the management-by-objectives concept is that it seems so obvious that most people believe they know how to do it. They have to learn from experience how difficult it is.

Some companies use management by objectives as a total approach to managing, rather than for some limited purpose such as appraising managerial performance, manpower planning, or compensation. Those using a total approach system claim that it is more effective. Whether your approach to management by objectives is limited or broad in scope, there are two concepts common to both: (1) The clearer the idea a manager has of what it is he is trying to achieve, the greater the chances of achieving it, and (2) his progress can be measured only in terms of what he is trying to make progress toward. At a recent AMA-sponsored workshop for top purchasing executives, a participant made a very strong recommendation for management by objectives. He said, "If you know where you want to go, you increase your chances of getting there. And if you have a list of objectives defined in terms of results to be achieved, you have a very solid notion of what an individual's job is."

Let's say you want to begin practicing management by objectives in your department regardless of whether other department heads do. How should you go about it? First, write down your major performance objective for the coming year and your specific plans, including target dates, for achieving these objectives. Second, submit them to your superior for review. Discuss them with him in detail. Be prepared to come out of the discussion with an agreed-upon set of objectives. Third, on a monthly, quarterly, or semiannual basis, review your progress toward these objectives with your superior. Revise and update them if needed. Fourth, at the end of the year prepare a report that lists all major achievements with comments on the variances between results actually achieved and results expected. Make this report as brief and to the point as possible. Fifth, submit this report to your superior and discuss it with him. Give him valid reasons why certain goals were not met. Sixth, establish a new set of objectives for the coming year.

WHAT MAKES MANAGEMENT BY OBJECTIVES WORK?

There is a lot of hard work for those responsible for carrying out a management-by-objectives program. The success of your program will depend upon the care and thoroughness with which your objectives are made, the vigorous persistence with which the program is followed, and the control that is exercised in watching progress, anticipating and removing obstacles, and updating the program if necessary.

The philosophy of purchasing management is oriented toward management by objectives. True, there are still many purchasing managers who are living in the old days and operating by the rule that materials should be purchased in the right quantity, be of the right quality, be at the right price, and be delivered at the right time. In most cases you will find that this purchasing manager is, in reality, an "order placer." He "never has the time" to practice management by objectives. The philosophy today is based on the concept of the commitment of company funds for on-schedule delivery of quality materials at acceptable prices. Total management planning and systems concepts are necessary for this commitment. Objectives established within such a climate have the ultimate aim of investing money for profit, not just saving money.

PROBLEMS OF THE APPROACH

In spite of its reported benefits, management by objectives is not without its problems and disadvantages. A case in point is that a manager may concentrate exclusively on achieving his own goals and neglect other areas of his responsibilities. A management-by-objectives program requires major changes before full benefits can be realized. Generally, however, most companies with a full-fledged management-by-objectives program claim that the benefits derived from such a program far outweigh any difficulties.

PURCHASING POLICY AND PROCEDURES

As a new purchasing manager one of the most important areas you will want to look at is purchasing policy, procedures, and controls. Just what do we mean by policies? You've certainly heard the phrase, "Sorry, it's company policy." This statement is used by management to say everything from "you can't have a raise" to "your new idea won't work." By using it as a perpetual negative answer to proposals, the manager is misinterpreting the business definition of the word "policy."

Many people confuse policies with rules. A rule allows no deviation, whereas a policy is a general description of a course of action. Perhaps this analogy will explain the difference:

Policies are like highways; they're guides to get you to your objective. You can go in any direction, but the paths are laid out for you. Rules, on the other hand, are stop signs or traffic lights to tell you when you can go and when you can't.

There are certain distinguishing features of policies that should be noted. They should reflect the department's objectives and plans. If they don't, why have them? They should be flexible. Goals change. If policies are disregarded often, take a look at them; they may be obsolete. They must leave room for discretion. Remember, they aren't rules. They can be widely interpreted, so they're not easy to control. They should be put in writing. This will force you to know your own policies well. They should be publicized throughout the department. If no one knows what your policies are, they're useless. Remember, it is imperative that they be reviewed and updated regularly.

Establishing procedures in your purchasing department, regardless of its size, is very important. By doing so you actually establish the status of the department in the company organization, the degree to which purchasing will be centralized, and the internal structure of the department itself. Such procedures outline the scope and functions of the purchasing department and necessitate the formulation of purchasing policies to cover such items as the quantity, price, and time of purchase, the selection of suppliers, and the form of purchase. You may wish to incorporate blanket orders for the purchase of highly repetitive items.

A policy must be clear and definitive if it is to be effective. An example of a basic purchasing policy is as follows:

1. The purchasing department has a primary purpose of conserving the time of operating departments whose personnel have other responsibilities.
2. Purchasing will initiate, conduct, and conclude all negotiations for materials and services.
3. All purchases must be made by the purchasing department.

4. Contacts with suppliers will be conducted with the knowledge and approval of the purchasing department.
5. Purchasing retains full authority to question the quality and type of materials requested for the purpose of protecting the best interests of the company.
6. All correspondence with suppliers must be made through the purchasing department, except in special cases, at which time copies of correspondence must be furnished to purchasing.
7. Requisitions must clearly define specifications and date delivery is required.
8. Purchasing will make every effort to locate two or more sources of supply.
9. All requests for samples must be routed through purchasing.
10. Employees are forbidden to accept gifts or gratuities, at any time, with a value in excess of five dollars ($5.00).

To function efficiently you will probably need several additional statements of policy. There should be a list of personnel who are authorized to sign requisitions; otherwise, unauthorized personnel may order material that either is not required or is for personal use. Another important point of policy would be to make clear who is responsible for your value analysis and standardization projects. You may want to establish a policy on visiting hours for salesmen. The basic problem is one of time. Salesmen have a certain amount of time for selling, and restrictions placed on their time cuts into their productive effort. On the other hand, a purchasing manager has other things to do besides talk to salesmen. There is no one answer to this problem; policies on visiting hours are handled in many ways, depending on the complexity of your company.

Policies regarding responsibility should recognize the close cooperation that must exist among engineering, production control, and purchasing personnel in determining what to buy, when to buy it, in what quantities to buy (minimum order quantity and the frequency of ordering), and how far ahead to commit the company. A similarly close coordination between affected departments is necessary even in companies not engaged in manufacturing. The objective should be to achieve the necessary cooperation and at the same time fix responsibility. In other areas, such as receiving material and processing invoices for payment, the policies should also fix responsibility and provide for appropriate internal controls.

Policies regarding sources of supply should establish standards that are to be met by all suppliers with which the company does a significant volume of business. These standards should cover such matters as reliability, reputation, financial soundness, and relationships with the company or its employees.

Price determination policies should cover such areas as competitive bidding, requests for price quotations, consideration of substitute materials, special consideration, if any, to be given to local sources or to customers, and attitude toward occasional "bargain" or "good buy" possibilities.

Policies covering the types of contractual obligations should express management's views as to the use of contracts, purchase orders, verbal orders, blanket orders, and so on. The methods of obligating the company may vary considerably with the type of business, the trade practice, and the nature of the purchases.

The problem of relationships with suppliers has always been somewhat difficult. Close cooperation is desirable in that it tends to improve the quality of product and the promptness of deliveries, to encourage the consideration of new ideas and methods, and to alleviate problems of product availability in times of limited supply. On the other hand, care must be exercised to avoid undue influence that may result from personal connections or loyalties. Some companies have recognized the desirability of a screening between key personnel of the companies and their significant suppliers. A good purchasing manager will make it a policy to require that purchases in excess of specified amounts be made only from suppliers on an "approved list." Procedures should be established for approval of supplier sources only after appropriate investigation. Whether there should be more than two sources of supply is a matter of judgment.

There are certain factors to be considered when approving a supplier. (1) Is the supplier honest and fair in his dealings with his customers? (2) Does he have adequate plant facilities to manufacture your quantity requirements? (3) Does he have the know-how that enables him to provide materials to meet your specifications? (4) Does he have a reputation for on-time delivery and service? (5) Is his financial position sound? (6) Are his prices competitive? In addition, the effective purchasing manager will determine whether the supplier's management policies are progressive; whether he is alert to the need for continued improvement in both his products and his manufacturing processes; and whether he realizes that in the final analysis his own interests are best served when he best serves his customers.

COMPETITIVE BIDDING

The knowledge of what prices are being charged by available sources of supply and the determination of what price you will pay is a very important part of your job as purchasing manager. After all, one of the primary objectives of purchasing is to obtain your requirements at the lowest ultimate cost. Ordinarily, competitive bidding is the most positive way of assuring advantageous prices. This means that you must obtain price quotations from various sources of supply. Most companies follow this practice to some degree, although a limited check of prices paid for highly repetitive items constitutes about all that is usually done.

The principle of "shopping around" is a sound one. As an effective purchasing manager you could well do more of this, tailoring the approach to fit your own situation. This may involve a combination of choices, such as formal competitive bidding on major purchases, continuous special studies of the cost of selected items on a rotating basis, and price-shopping on certain types of purchases. At any rate, as purchasing manager you should have a competitive bidding policy for the guidance of your personnel or for your own use in the event yours is a one-man operation.

Other special situations in purchasing involve such areas as considerations to be given to local suppliers and reciprocal relationships with customers of the company. Although such relationships may be considered under certain circumstances, it is important that exceptions to normal procedures and arm's length purchasing policies be established by the purchasing manager and approved by the highest level of management, and that the possible benefits be weighed carefully against the costs.

Another special situation for the purchasing manager is the make-or-buy decision. Although this question generally is not associated with the purchasing function, behind many purchase orders there are decisions to buy rather than to make the items. The purchasing manager can be of immense assistance to the production personnel in this regard.

The purchasing manager should also establish a policy with respect to "accommodation purchases" for employees so as to avoid misunderstandings and possible abuses.

In conclusion, a policy statement by the purchasing manager serves several purposes. It provides a guide for purchasing personnel, it sets standards that reduce the number of executive decisions, and it establishes the authority and responsibility of the purchasing function within the company.

PURCHASING TECHNIQUES

Certainly, as a new purchasing manager, one of the first things you will want to do is determine what purchasing techniques you will establish. Unfortunately, in many small companies purchasing is a basic, routine, and often haphazard function; yet it is the most vital function of all in terms of impact on profit. New techniques are being used today to improve the efficiency of the purchasing function and to realize the maximum contribution to profit. In the average company, cost of materials purchased accounts for upward of fifty cents out of each sales dollar, while profit is represented by about five cents of the sales dollar. This means that as little as a 1 percent cost reduction in purchasing could result in as much as a 10 percent increase in profit return.

As purchasing manager you can make a good impression on management by letting it be known that your aim is to maximize efficiency in the purchasing department by achieving the lowest possible cost consistent with customer requirements. This is done by purchasing the right quantity at the right time and at the right price, from the right source, for delivery at the right time. Of course you must produce results, not just words in this endeavor, and this will demand highly effective and, often, very fast decision making on your part. In many cases, purchasing is but one of the hats you will wear in a small company.

ECONOMIC ORDER QUANTITY DETERMINATION

One of the more important techniques used today is known as EOQ (economic order quantity). Some prefer EPQ (economic purchase quantity). Economic order determination has generally been hindered by the fears of purchasing people and some suppliers who are traditionally interested in maximizing order quantities. These fears are really unfounded, particularly in light of the simple methods now available for determining economic order quantities. The fundamentals of reliable, easy EOQ determination are simple; they do not require a great knowledge of accounting, economics, mathematics, inventory management, production planning, or other managerial principles to be understood.

EOQ is simply a fundamental plan, applied consistently over a long period, that insures the purchase of the right quantity, at the right price, and at the lowest possible cost. Specifically, EOQ is the order quantity that results in the lowest annual cost, taking into consideration such interrelated elements as quantity discounts, the cost of preparation and processing of purchase orders, and the cost of carrying inventory. This concept promises the greatest potential benefit for the average company, because it provides the means to insure the best possible balance between the two primary objectives of the purchasing function:

1. To have sufficient merchandise available to meet customer requirements.
2. To minimize the costs of purchasing by careful attention to vital elements of economic inventory levels, to savings available through volume purchases, and to possible savings in the cost of processing purchase orders.

EOQ determination involves analyzing annual usage of merchandise purchased, costs of processing a purchase order, costs of carrying the merchandise in inventory, and multiple price-quantity combinations. The principal significance of EOQ revolves around the high costs of carrying inventories and, of course, the high cost of lost sales that occur when required merchandise is not in inventory. For example, accountants tell us that the cost of carrying inventory averages about 35 percent per year of the average inventory value. In a typical small company we can assume a comparable rate of inventory usage. This means that the annual cost of carrying inventory can be as much as 35 percent of one-half the dollar value of an order. In other words, a purchase order for merchandise with a total purchase value of $600 could cost as much as $105 in inventory carrying expense on an annual basis.

The objective of an EOQ determination is to reduce this substantial inventory carrying cost to a minimum and, at the same time, earn the best possible quantity discount from the supplier and achieve the lowest possible expense in the preparation and processing of purchase orders.

The EOQ formula can be expressed as follows: Total Annual Cost = Number of Orders × (Purchase Order Cost + Inventory Carrying Cost + Cost of Processing Purchase Orders). To determine EOQ, a sequence of steps must be followed.

1. To provide the purchase order cost for use in the formula, the purchase price is multiplied by the purchase quantity. This is a simple extension of unit cost-by-order-quantity, based on a selected price-discount combination available from the supplier.

2. Daily usage of the merchandise is determined by subtracting the last order date from the current order date and dividing the difference, in days, into the last order quantity. The estimated number of days' supply represented by the current order is then obtained by dividing the daily usage into the order quantity.

3. The purchase order cost (unit price × quantity as determined in Step 1) is multiplied by 35 percent (the average annual cost of carrying inventory) to provide the inventory carrying cost of the order.

4. The purchase order cost and the inventory carrying cost for the order are added together. To this amount, a standard sum, which represents the cost of processing an order, must be added. The standard cost of processing a purchase order is an estimated figure. It takes into consideration management and clerical time involved in developing and preparing the purchase order, clerical and accounting costs involved in issuing and following up an order, and the physical handling cost involved in receiving an order, checking quantity, and moving the merchandise into inventory.

Although we noted that the standard cost of processing a purchase order is based on an estimate, the estimate should be as realistic as possible. Once established, this standard cost of processing an order should be applied universally in EOQ determination.

5. After the purchase order cost, cost of carrying inventory, and cost of processing an order are totaled, the number of days' supply (as determined in step 2) is divided into 365. This is done to obtain the number of purchase orders annually at the given order quantity.

6. The number of orders annually is multiplied by the sum of the purchase order cost, inventory carrying cost, and order processing cost to provide the total annual cost for the given order quantity at the given price.

By repeating this process for each of several price-discount combinations available from the supplier and comparing the total annual cost figures, you can determine the EOQ for the merchandise. Once the EOQ is established, it can be maintained and applied as long as there is no change in the supplier price-quantity discount structure or in the usage rates of the merchandise. You may find that by using the EOQ formula you will lower your purchasing cost and contribute proportionately to the profit picture, on an annual basis, by placing fewer orders for larger quantities. On the other hand, the EOQ formula might show up a fallacy in trying for the largest volume discount at the expense of excessive inventory carrying costs.

The use of the EOQ leads to a sound philosophy of purchasing policy and procedure. In summary, a sound system of EOQ applied either to individual items or broadly to a class of items will provide both direct and intangible benefits and will save a recognizable sum in terms of invested capital, financial charges, storage space, and purchasing expenditures. Intelligent use of historical data will frequently suggest groupings of items having similar EOQ characteristics, which can then be coded; this will avoid repetition of individual calculations. These savings might justify a continuing expenditure of time and payroll for maximum results, but many companies operate this function on an intermittent basis. In your new job as purchasing manager it will pay to survey the need, train your personnel, and apply these principles to those limited situations where the main saving is to be attained.

Another technique the purchasing manager should put to use is a work simplification program. In fact, such a program should be in continuous operation. Most purchasing managers have found that no one system will do the job; they use a combination of systems. A list of some of the results a good work simplification program has achieved follows:

- Materials have been obtained sooner at lower costs.
- Suppliers have had their record keeping simplified and have received help in inventory planning.
- Accounting work has been reduced by having fewer invoices to process and fewer checks to write.
- A large part of repetitive purchasing work has been handled in minimum time, giving the purchasing manager and buyers a great opportunity to concentrate on the search for better deals, better service, and better materials.

The purchasing manager of a small company would do well to direct his work simplification program to reducing effort on repetitive buying. There are a variety of methods that can be used, including the following: (1) blanket orders, (2) the use of requisitions as purchase orders, and (3) the purchase history card.

Blanket orders are most useful when it is not feasible to list quantities because of the highly repetitive nature of the item being purchased. For example, in the vending and food service industry we use the blanket purchase order for the purchase of dairy products, pastry items, automotive parts, and many other "daily" items. An industrial purchasing manager could do equally well using the blanket order for buying fasteners, tubes, nuts and bolts, and so on. The blanket purchase order merely lists the description of the item and the price agreed upon for a specified period of time. The order should also indicate the complete terms of the contract between the buyer and seller.

The use of requisitions as purchase orders is a good way for the purchasing manager to reduce paperwork. If the requisitioner has properly entered the need on a form, you can forward it to the supplier as his authorization to ship the material. Thus you will save time spent in typing purchase orders and distributing copies throughout the company. It is obvious that this method can be used only on a limited number of items such as office supplies and perhaps other small value items. It is, of course, necessary for you to work out the details of such a program with the supplier as well as with your own accounting personnel.

The purchase history card is used by many companies. It is usually printed on card stock and serves the dual purpose of stock record and requisition to purchase. Many companies call this a traveling requisition. For items that are regularly stocked or frequently purchased, a purchase history card is used to reduce repetitive writing of requisitions, necessitating only such entries as quantity and date ordered.

Other ways to eliminate typed purchase orders should not be overlooked by the purchasing manager. For example: Can you use signed packing slips as receiving reports? Can you approve invoices instead of prepricing orders? (This method isn't recommended for a large company.) Can you make use of work already being satisfactorily done—and properly so—by another area of your company? Can you eliminate work now being done that is consistently repeated?

Other purchasing techniques are discussed in more detail elsewhere in this book; however, this may well be the place for you as the new purchasing manager to audit your operation by asking, "Is my purchasing operation open to kickbacks?" For example, if you answer no to two of the following questions, your operation is weak on controls. On the other hand, if your answer is no to *more* than two questions you are wide open for corruption and must begin policing your purchasing techniques at once.

1. Are at least three people involved in purchasing procedures—in evaluating and specifying purchases?
2. Do you ask for competitive bids on special equipment?
3. Do you have a policy of dealing with more than one supplier on an identical item?
4. Are your procedures audited at least once each year?
   (a) By an internal auditor.
   (b) By an external auditor.
5. Do you maintain a periodic check on employees who have a great deal of authority?
6. Do you have a firm policy about
   (a) Gifts?
   (b) Entertainment?

With reference to the foregoing list, there are six common faults that auditors usually find when checking purchasing operations in a small company:

- Lack of control.
- Lack of an economical small order system.
- Unpriced purchase orders.
- Lack of billing information.
- Absence of the terms of the contract.
- Insufficient use of blanket orders.

In summary, as purchasing manager you have the opportunity to play the leading role in the development of sound purchasing techniques. The specific strategies will vary considerably from company to company; for example, the programs of a company engaged in the resale or assembly of materials will be different from those of a company engaged in manufacturing.

SMALL ORDER PROBLEM

It is doubtful whether there is a purchasing manager or buyer anywhere who likes small orders. In fact, small orders are disliked by sales as well as purchasing personnel, because they claim that these orders waste both time and money. The small order problem is faced by small and large companies alike, but nothing seems to be done to solve the problem.

What is a small order? There is no simple answer to this question. Each purchasing manager will classify his purchase orders into the small category on the basis of his own company's operations. There are, however, two rather common criteria that have been applied—dollar value and importance of the item. Perhaps all purchasing managers would agree that a transaction that has a low dollar value, involves only a few items, and can be purchased in a routine manner should be classified as a small order.

Dollar value is generally considered to be the most important single factor in classifying a given purchase order as small. This is its value in terms of the total transaction rather than just unit price. Dollar value can be measured precisely, and a direct comparison can be made between the cost of materials on an order and the cost of placing that order. A basic concern with small orders is the question of *what it costs to spend a dollar.*

Small orders are also identified on the basis of the importance of the item in maintaining uninterrupted manufacturing operations as well as in maintaining an adequate inventory of office supplies. Thus when a relatively unimportant item is purchased it is classified as a small order.

However, many companies do not classify an item crucial to continued operations as a small order, regardless of the dollar value or the quantity purchased. The importance of an item does not necessarily have a high degree of correlation with its value. For example, one small maintenance item worth $5.00 can become quite critical and important if its absence results in closing down a major piece of equipment on a production line. True, the $5.00 value would clearly place the item in the small order category, but the need—because of potential shutdown costs—is so great that the cost of placing a purchase order becomes insignificant by comparison.

What Is the Small Order Problem?

In its simplest terms, the problem associated with small orders is the cost incurred in processing a purchase order. It is usually difficult to justify a situation where the cost of buying an item is greater than the cost of the item itself. This, then, is the problem—*how to keep purchasing costs in a reasonable relationship to the value of the item being purchased.* To better understand the magnitude of the problem it is necessary to look at the types of costs that are included in purchasing cost and to determine in what way these costs are affected by placing small purchase orders.

Buyer's time. The purchasing manager or buyer must spend a certain amount of time on every requisition received. This time is not necessarily directly correlated to the size of the purchase. As a matter of fact, it may be that more time is actually spent on a smaller purchase. When a small order involves a nonrepetitive, infrequently purchased item, the buyer may not be able to rely on memory or records of previous purchases to quickly establish a potential source. He may have to do considerable seeking before a source is located and evaluated. Thus time spent in this manner on small orders may well be at the expense of time that could be devoted to larger or more important purchase orders. Additionally, small orders create as big a work load in receiving and accounts payable as do large orders, unless a special system is developed for processing such orders.

Freight costs. Since most commercial transportation firms operate under a minimum weight and/or size system of rates, it is inevitable that freight costs relative to the value of small orders are likely to be completely out of line as compared with such costs on a large order.

Unit prices. Many costs connected with processing a purchase order at a supplier's place of business are relatively fixed regardless of the value of the transaction. As a result, suppliers are forced into the practice of establishing a minimum charge price system with a high base but with significant discounts as the quantity purchased is increased. Since it is almost impossible to do any price negotiating on a small order, the buyer for a small company cannot take advantage of these discounts. In many instances it seems that when a requisition covering a small order is received, the purchasing manager disposes of it in the quickest and easiest manner, which is likely to result in no real search for the lowest unit price available.

There are a number of possible targets that can be established in the search for a solution to the small order problem. It is necessary that you, the purchasing manager, consider all these areas in attempting to solve the problem. Included among these are (1) reduced time spent in source searching; (2) reduced clerical work in the purchasing, receiving, warehouse, accounts payable, and cost accounting offices; (3) reduced freight costs; and (4) reduced suppliers' selling, handling, shipping, and billing costs.

CLASSIFICATION OF SMALL ORDERS

Purchase orders within the small order category can be divided into two basic classifications: recurring and nonrecurring. Recurring small orders offer greater potential for cost savings than nonrecurring orders, simply because there are more such orders. Although it is difficult to reduce the volume of either class of small orders, there remains a challenge to reduce procedural costs, and the greatest opportunity for this is in the reduction of paperwork.

The recurring purchase. The small order for items being purchased on a recurring basis offers the greatest possibility for instituting procedural improvements. Systems can be developed that will enable you to process them in a routine manner. As you well know, any business activity that can be handled in a routine manner rather than being treated as a special case can be handled more economically. Blanket purchase orders, group purchasing, the traveling requisition or purchase history card, the "out" card, and the purchasing of service are all possibilities for solving this problem.

Blanket purchase orders. This subject is covered elsewhere in this book. However, it is important to point out that a blanket purchase order may be the system best suited for your small order repetitive purchases.

Group purchasing. Group purchasing, sometimes called "family buying" or "consolidated purchasing," refers to the practice of consolidating like items or items that can be secured from a single source for purchase at the same time. This method helps to reduce the volume of small orders by combining a number of items on a single purchase order rather than issuing a series of separate orders.

One approach under the group purchasing procedure is to review all items that fall within the same group at the time a requisition for a single item in that group is written. Although this procedure results in an increase of time expended on reviewing inventory levels, it will be more than offset by the reduction in the number of separate requisitions and purchase orders. This system, when used with blanket orders, will also reduce the number of releases against the blanket order. Additionally, there is a work reduction in receiving and accounts payable. The supplier gains also in that he is able to include many items on a single packing slip, in the same shipment, and on the same invoice.

The traveling requisition or purchase history card. A traveling requisition or purchase history card (Exhibit 1) moves back and forth between the stores department and the purchasing department. When the order point is reached in the stores department, the traveling requisition is forwarded to the purchasing department. Purchasing makes the appropriate entries indicating placement of the order on the requisition and returns it to the stores department. The stores department posts issues and receipts on it until the next order point is reached and the cycle begins again.

The principal advantage of the purchase history card is that it reduces the time required by the stores department to write

Exhibit 1
The Purchase History Card

the Macke company

RECURRING PURCHASE HISTORY

CO. NO. _____ BRANCH _____

LOCATION _____

BIN _____

	SUPPLIERS	ACCOUNTING NUMBER	CATALOG NUMBER	DESCRIPTION
A				CATALOG AND PURCHASE ORDER DESCRIPTION _____
B				
C				MAKE AND MODEL — QUANTITY REQ'D FOR STOCK
D				UNIT — STANDARD PACKAGE

SHOP STOREKEEPER / OPERATIONS

SHOP STOREKEEPER				OPERATIONS								PURCHASING RECORD						SHOP STOREKEEPER		
Date	On Hand	Quan. to Order	Stores Approval	Max.	Min.	Approval	Supplier	Price	Per	Terms	FOB	Order Date	Order Number	Destination				Quan. Rec'd.	Date Rec'd.	Rec'd. By
TOTAL																				

PURCHASING 6070

requisitions and by the purchasing department to look up past purchase records. Cost reduction is thereby achieved primarily by the elimination of a lot of clerical work.

The "out" card. Where there are a number of traveling requisitions or purchase history cards and a likelihood that someone in stores will think that the requisition was lost, an out card (Exhibit 2) is used. At the time a traveling requisition is pulled from the file and sent to purchasing, an out card is put in its place. A clerk merely notes the same part number on the out card as is shown on the traveling requisition.

Exhibit 2
The Out Card

Original Card OUT, forwarded to PURCHASING

PART NO.	DATE REMOVED	BY WHOM	PURPOSE

2720

The purchasing of service. A purchasing manager is frequently involved in the purchasing of services, particularly in connection with the repair and maintenance of equipment. This requirement is often of an unexpected nature and results in a series of purchase orders at irregular intervals. Ordinarily, this type of purchasing is handled in one of three ways. (1) A service contract is entered into for a specified period of time—usually annually. (2) A separate purchase order is issued each time service is required. (3) No purchase order is issued; invoices are approved after each service call.

In the opinion of many of us, it is foolish to enter into a service contract on office machines less than two years old. Regardless of the procedure adopted for handling service requirements, however, the objective of a solution to this type of small order problem is to reduce both the number of invoices from the supplier and your own paperwork.

The nonrecurring purchase. The small order for the nonrecurring type of purchase differs in one marked respect from the recurring type of purchase—it is impossible to develop a system that will concentrate such purchases and thereby increase the value of the transaction in relation to the handling costs incurred. Any solution, however, will have the objective of reducing to a minimum the cost of spending a dollar without impairing the services. In some instances, it may be necessary to break with traditional accounting practice to achieve this objective. Several methods for accomplishing this reduction in cost are discussed here. They include the use of petty cash, C.O.D. orders, telephone orders, and immediate payment by check.

Petty cash. Since petty cash is a sum of money set aside to meet minor expenses, wouldn't it be logical to use petty cash to pay for small orders? What could be more simple than paying cash for a one-time purchase and thereby eliminating all the paperwork? The petty cash system offers the primary advantage of reducing the cost of paying for small orders. For accounting control, a sales slip can be used as a receiving document along with the petty cash voucher.

The petty cash fund for small purchases should be under the control of the purchasing manager to insure the advantages of centralized purchasing. Granting petty cash funds to other departments will be giving them a license to buy directly. This will result in waste, because one department may purchase an item directly that another department requisitions regularly. In addition, rush orders tend to be encouraged because of the simplicity of the pick-up and payment system. Unless they are controlled by purchasing, petty cash orders usually forfeit cash discounts.

C.O.D. orders. Companies that do not permit C.O.D. orders may well find that relaxing this rule will reduce cost. If C.O.D. fees are involved, it becomes a matter of comparing the C.O.D. fee with the cost of processing payment in the conventional manner. In many instances, the fee will be the lesser of the two. By providing C.O.D. payments for the cost of materials, for the cost of freight, or for both, the work of the accounts payable department is reduced.

Telephone orders. In most cases, nonrecurring small orders require the purchasing manager to determine price and availability. A number of innovations can be applied to a telephone order. For example, a four-part form can be used for the requisition, purchase order, receiving report, and invoice. When the purchasing manager receives this form, properly filled out, he telephones the supplier. No written order is forwarded. Neither does the supplier receive any copies of the form. When the materials are received, accounting uses one part for the invoice and payment is rapid.

It is important that the following limitations be made applicable to telephone orders:

- Delivery must be within 30 days.
- Orders shipped must be complete; back orders will not be accepted.
- There will be no payment for overshipment.
- There is a maximum dollar limitation.

Payment by check. An unconventional innovation to reduce

the cost of nonrepetitive small orders is to include a check along with the purchase order. In fact, the check is actually a part of the purchase order. It is drawn on a special revolving fund and included as a detachable stub on the purchase order. Invoices are thus eliminated completely. Obviously, a maximum dollar limit is established under this procedure and we must assume that both parties to this type of transaction are trustworthy and reliable.

To summarize, in the case of small orders for *nonrecurring* types of items, you should make every effort to minimize the costs connected with the handling of such orders. The request itself cannot be eliminated, but if several steps in the purchasing process can be combined or bypassed, savings can be effected. The greatest opportunity for effecting economies is in connection with the steps involved in the payment for such purchases.

Small orders for a *recurring* type of purchase can be handled in a number of ways that minimize the cost and reduce the size of this problem. For example, planning and scheduling can reduce such small orders by combining several of them into a single transaction. And, too, special arrangements for combining invoices on the part of the supplier can reduce the paperwork ordinarily connected with handling a large volume of invoices.

You may find the following three steps helpful in solving your small order problem:

1. Analyze and categorize your purchase orders over a specified period of time to determine whether they should be classed as small orders or whether they should have been combined with others for single source purchasing.

2. Determine whether any procedure can be adopted that will reduce costs for handling such orders in terms of the clerical function within purchasing and the clerical or operating functions within other departments of the company.

3. Don't be afraid to depart from traditional practices. Exercise ingenuity in proposing and testing alternative procedures for handling your small orders.

THE PURCHASE ORDER SYSTEM

The question of what the proper design of a purchase order system for a small company should be is a difficult one. After much thought, the system used by *The Evening Star Newspaper Company*, Washington, D.C. was chosen as an outstanding model. Permission to use the material in this section has been granted to the author by Leonard A. Larson, Purchasing Officer of the *Star* and a long-time personal friend. Mr. Larson is a past president of the Purchasing Management Association of Washington, D.C., and one of the finest professional purchasing managers in the country.

All of us realize that procedures and forms vary considerably from company to company. This is to be expected, since no two firms operate exactly alike. Because of these differences, it would be extremely difficult to suggest a universally acceptable system that would meet the requirements of every type of business. The objective of this section is not to attempt to offer a solution to all problems, but to rekindle interest in what to most of us is a very basic tool in any purchasing operation, namely, the purchase order. The emphasis will be on its effectiveness as a communications device and a transaction control.

It is evident that emphasis currently is being placed upon various forms of automated data processing systems for the efficient handling of most business functions. These methods are wonderful, if technological skill and practical necessity can be economically combined. According to many who have survived the change-over to EDP systems, much time and expense can be saved if existing manual systems are refined and thoroughly understood before an attempt is made to select or modify proposed automated methods.

With this thought in mind, let's review a simple system used to convert a once haphazard situation into an orderly process. The flow chart in Exhibit 3 represents the order of events in a typical manual purchasing cycle. The cycle illustrated here has eight control points. We shall review these points to fa-

Exhibit 3
Purchasing Procedure

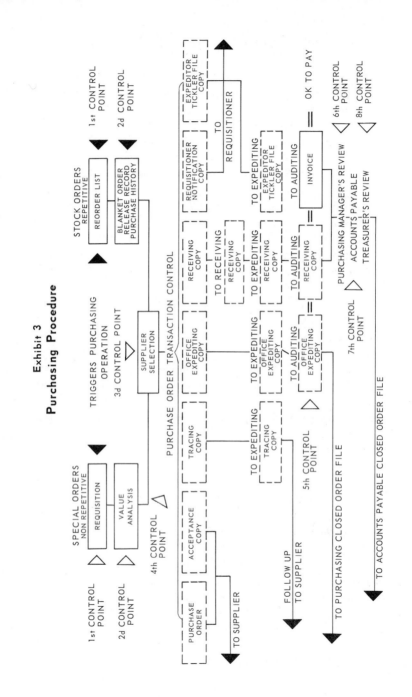

miliarize you with the environment in which the purchase order system that is under review operates. After seeing where and how the purchase order functions in the whole purchasing system, we'll review the form in more detail and discuss the transaction controls that are built into it.

The simple procedure outlined in the flow chart recognizes two main categories of purchases: nonrepetitive special orders and repetitive stocked supply items. The special orders are handled on individually placed purchase orders, and the stock replacement purchases are managed on blanket purchase orders.

The first point of control is exercised at the requisition level. Because this function actually triggers the purchasing operation, it is closely regulated by a formal requisition authority. This limits the number of people having authority to request purchases to be made and serves to cut down the otherwise tremendous number of costly nuisance requests that would arrive at the purchasing department. All requisitions are written and must bear an authorized signature before they can be processed.

Stock items are managed by the purchasing department, which is its own requisition authority for this class of purchase. It also is responsible for inventory control and for the receiving, stocking, issuing, auditing, and certification of invoices for payment by the accounting department.

The second point of control is the value analysis check, which is performed by the buyer or purchasing manager. The value of administrative time as well as of the product is of interest. Each requisition is checked for proper authorization and completeness of specifications before any further action takes place. If information is lacking, clarification is sought. If the specifications are highly restrictive, the requisitioner is urged to help lower costs and speed delivery by using competitively available standard items. Whenever possible, the purchasing department renders prerequisitioning assistance to other department heads in locating the best practical solutions to supply and equipment requirements.

The stock items, which are controlled by blanket purchase orders, are competitively sourced, and estimated requirements for a twelve-month period are covered. Each item has its own purchase history record upon which numbered telephone releases are placed. All that remains in terms of value analysis during the life of the blanket order is to judge the economic order quantity to be released each time the reorder point has been reached. EOQ formulas or less sophisticated techniques for determining space use and expenditures can be utilized at this point.

The third point of control is at the time of supplier selection, which consists of the usual evaluation of competitive bids or analysis of individual proposals to determine order placement.

The fourth point of control is the purchase order and its related parts, which regulate the mechanics of a transaction. This is the specific area to which the subject matter in this section is directed. It will be examined in more detail later. Please note the prominence of this form in the chart of the entire system.

The fifth point of control is the verification of equality between the original requirement (represented by the office copy of the purchase order), the actual performance (represented by the executed receiving copy of the purchase order), and the audited invoices, as a prerequisite to payment of the invoice. As long as the formula is satisfied, routine administrative procedures are sufficient to close the transaction. If the formula is not satisfied, the invoice is not paid until the inequalities have been properly resolved.

When the transaction is closed in the purchasing department, proof of complete and proper handling is in evidence on the receiving copy of the purchase order. It accompanies the invoice as proof that the bill is payable as certified by the purchasing department.

The sixth point of control is the purchasing manager's review of the transaction to be sure it has been handled properly before it continues its procedure for payment and final closing process. As purchasing manager, you can elect to review each transaction, or you may request that you be alerted to the exceptions only. This promotes flexibility and permits varying degrees of control without altering the system to achieve it.

The seventh point of control is the accounts payable preparation of the check and the posting of any records required by their processes.

The eighth point of control is the treasurer's review of the transaction and the actual signing of the check for payment. If he desires to examine each transaction before signing the check for payment, a complete management report on each transaction is present in the form of the executed receiving report. With this complete purchase order control, nothing can be hidden from the treasurer or auditors. Documentation is complete and thorough and justifies all purchases made as well as invoices paid. The receiving report with the invoice attached is then filed in the accounts payable closed order file for future reference or review by anyone having the need.

So there you have a relatively simple acquisition cycle used by many small- to medium-size companies. This particular system is used by a company with a purchasing department consisting of seven people—a purchasing manager, two buyers, an expediter who also serves as an invoice auditor, a secretary, and two shipping and receiving clerks. It differs from some purchasing operations in that the purchasing department is also responsible for inventory control, stocking, issuing, and checking invoices. The desire to regulate is quite obvious in this system. There are no petty cash or systems contracting procedures in use because of the possibility of losing individual transaction control.

With respect to the system just described, please bear in mind that there are several schools of thought on paperwork in the purchasing functions these days. Some people view paperwork as a distasteful chore that impedes the progress of their business. They proceed to cut corners to the extent that their business processes eventually are inadequately documented and individual transactions rest on highly perishable verbal agreements. Those who uphold this philosophy are foolish. It may appear that a few dollars would be saved in printed forms and processing time, but the frequency of errors and duplication of effort created without this system would be far more costly. Regardless of our individual viewpoints on paperwork, most of us will agree that inadequate or incomplete communications cause a large amount of wasted time and expense in our day-to-day business operations.

THE PURCHASE ORDER

Now that we have reviewed the environment in which the purchase order operates, let's examine the form itself in some detail. A properly designed order form can be an efficient communication device that will save time and expense in the long run. It is, without question, a vital part of an efficient purchasing system. Each part of the purchase order form has its function; it assigns and documents the responsibility for performance at each step of the process. Herein lies its strength and value as a business procedure.

A purchase order is the legal authorization to a supplier to furnish goods or services as indicated. It should, therefore, be written in such a fashion that upon acceptance it represents total agreement between the supplier and the buyer in completely understandable terms. This is a skill that all buyers and purchasing managers should develop. It will insure promptness and accuracy in the filling of an order. Furthermore, the form assigns a serial number (P.O. number) to each transaction, which permits instant identification and processing of goods and paperwork. The processing time saved by this simple feature is tremendous and very often overlooked by those who are opposed to formal purchase order systems.

In the event of disagreement concerning any aspect of a transaction, the purchase order, if properly designed and used, becomes the basic document referred to in settling disputes. There is no need to try to recall what the spoken word was or to engage in arguments based on vague recollections, especially when lead times are lengthy and confusion is at an all-time high because of shortages and general supplier carelessness in the filling of orders.

The Purchase Order form, Exhibit 4, is designed to insure that there is ample space for data required. The top third contains the customary identifying information. The supplier's address space is properly designated by printed brackets, which insures that the address will be correctly placed so that it will show through the window of a standard #10 glassine envelope. The single horizontal rule below the line of captions, beginning with the term "Item No.," is the fold line. This reference and the brackets insure that no hand addressing of envelopes will have to be made by the post office. The time saved by this little precaution is quite obvious. The shipping instructions, in addition to the addresses, are clearly defined to insure that shipments do not arrive marked with the company address only. If this occurs, particularly on small packages, they can easily go astray in the plant and be lost for several days.

Items such as the purchase order number, date, ship via, FOB point, and delivery date are standard captions. There is, however, an unusual provision in the "terms" block. This one reads "Terms—discounted from receiving date unless otherwise specified." Discounting from the invoice date, which is customary, would often result in having to pay the invoice prior to delivery in order to earn the discount. In this instance, this is not done unless agreed to as a condition of sale. The acceptance of the order by the supplier automatically insures his agreement with this provision and prevents the loss of many term discounts.

You will note that the buyer must also show the name and telephone number of the person he has contacted at the supplier's office. This is a real time saver in that it insures that orders will get into the proper hands to begin with. It also means that any member of the purchasing department who is placed in a position of "picking up the marbles" on an order can do so without having to waste time trying to find out the name and

Exhibit 4
Purchase Order — Original Copy

Purchase Order

The Evening Star Newspaper Co.
2ND & VIRGINIA AVE., S. E.
WASHINGTON, D. C.   20003

No. 62082

DATE ___ June 11, 1970

TERMS - DISCOUNTED FROM RECEIVING DATE UNLESS OTHERWISE SPECIFIED.

SHIP VIA	F.O.B.	DELIVERY DATE	
Local Delivery	Delivered	July 9, 1970	Net 30 Days

TO

A Lithograph Company
Main Street
U. S. A.

Attention: Mr. John Doe
(301) 555-1212

SHIP TO

UNLESS OTHERWISE STATED IN ORDER, SHIP TO ABOVE ADDRESS

ATTENTION PURCHASING
RECEIVING DEPT. 2nd FLOOR
STOCK CLERK

ITEM NO.	QUANTITY	BILLS PAYABLE ONLY UPON COMPLETION OF ORDER		UNIT	TOTAL
1.	6,000	1971 STAR CALENDARS			$3,072.12
		Copy:	Herewith, camera ready, prints two sides different copy on 7 pages. Insert 12 half-tones where indicated. No bleeds.	sales tax	122.88
					$3,195.00
		Stock:	130 M White Frosty Afton Cover		
		Size:	13'' x 19''		
		Size:	13'' x 19''		
		Ink:	Blue — Lewis Roberts 458 Green — Capico Speed Match PMS 390		
		Collate:	Per Dummy		
		Binding:	White plastic binding approx. 12'' long. Bind on the 13'' side at top.		
		Drill:	Each calendar with 1/4'' hole in top center, below binding.		
		Proof:	No		
		Wrap:	25 calendars per package and mark each package.		

INSTRUCTIONS TO VENDOR

1. USE OUR ACCEPTANCE FORM.
2. SUPPLY DATA REQUESTED ON ACCEPTANCE COPY AND RETURN AT ONCE.
3. ADVISE IMMEDIATELY ANY DELAYS IN ORDER COMPLETION OR SHIPPING.
4. INVOICES, CORRESPONDENCE, AND SHIPPING CONTAINERS MUST SHOW OUR P.O. NO.
5. ADDRESS INVOICES AND CORRESPONDENCE TO PURCHASING OFFICER.

For The Evening Star Newspaper Company

BY _Sample_

SAMPLER   PURCHASING OFFICER

Exhibit 4 — Continued

Acceptance Copy

CORRECT ALL PRICING ERRORS AND SUPPLY MISSING PRICES.	VENDOR FURNISH ALL INFORMATION
	1. COMPLETE SHIPMENT WILL MOVE ON — DATE _____
	2. VIA _____
	3. ACKNOWLEDGED BY _____ TITLE _____
EXPLAIN DELAY OR PARTIAL SHIPMENTS ON REVERSE SIDE.	4. PHONE NUMBER _____ CITY _____
	5. DATE OF THIS ACKNOWLEDGMENT _____

Tracing Copy

ACKNOWLEDGEMENT OF THIS ORDER DATED _____

INDICATED THAT ☐ PARTIAL SHIPMENT ☐ COMPLETE SHIPMENT

WOULD BE MADE ON _____

BY _____ TITLE _____

PHONE _____

VENDOR FURNISH ALL INFORMATION

☐ COMPLETE SHIPMENT WILL BE MADE AS PROMISED.
☐ SHIPMENT WILL NOT BE MADE AS PROMISED (EXPLAIN ON REVERSE)

BY _____ TITLE _____

PHONE NUMBER _____

Office Copy

Pro...

Wrap: 25 calendars per package and mark each package.

QUOTES:

1. Ajax Talbot Litho. = $3072.12
2. Supreme Printing = $3250.00
3. Webester's Press = $3382.00
4. Mark Fray Co. = $4060.00
5. Austin Printers = $4728.00

Notify: Sue Miller, Ext. 789 when in.
Stockroom: Store in 4th floor storeroom until called for.
CHARGE: Advertising Promotion Printing

INVOICE AMOUNT	$3195.00				
INVOICE NO.	7019				
INVOICE DATE	7-9-70				
DATE PASSED	7-15-70				

Reverse Side of Office Copy

EXPEDITING NOTES

DATE	
6-22-70	Jack said he can only give us a small partial tomorrow, will deliver balance in daily increments as they come out of bindery.
6-30-70	Sue needs these as soon as possible to get mailing started. Call Jack to ask him to give us larger quantities as soon as possible.
7-3-70	Jack called and said last partial due tomorrow or Monday.

Exhibit 4 — Concluded

Receiving Copy

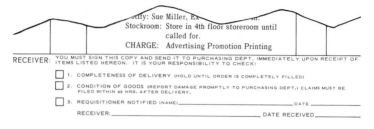

...tify: Sue Miller, Ex...
Stockroom: Store in 4th floor storeroom until
called for.
CHARGE: Advertising Promotion Printing

RECEIVER: YOU MUST SIGN THIS COPY AND SEND IT TO PURCHASING DEPT. IMMEDIATELY UPON RECEIPT OF
ITEMS LISTED HEREON. IT IS YOUR RESPONSIBILITY TO CHECK:

- [ ] 1. COMPLETENESS OF DELIVERY (HOLD UNTIL ORDER IS COMPLETELY FILLED)
- [ ] 2. CONDITION OF GOODS (REPORT DAMAGE PROMPTLY TO PURCHASING DEPT.) CLAIMS MUST BE FILED WITHIN 48 HRS. AFTER DELIVERY.
- [ ] 3. REQUISITIONER NOTIFIED (NAME)_____ DATE _____

RECEIVER:_____ DATE RECEIVED_____

Reverse Side of Receiving Copy

RECEIVING AND ISSUING DATA
SPECIAL ORDERS OR PARTIAL ORDERS

STOCK CLERK RECEIVING RECORD   STOCK CLERK ISSUING RECORD

ITEM NO.	QUANTITY RECEIVED	RECEIVED BY	PERSON NOTIFIED	DATE NOTIFIED	QUANTITY PICKED UP	PICKED UP BY	DATE DELIVERED OR PICKED UP	DEL. BY	DEL. TO
1	300	S B	Jackson	6-23-70	300	S. Miller	6-23-70		
1	750	S B	S. Miller	6-25-70	750	S. Miller	6-25-70		
1	1750	S B	S. Miller	6-26-70	1750	S. Miller	6-26-70		
1	1025	S B	S. Miller	6-29-70	1025	S. Miller	6-29-70		
1	1400	S B	S. Miller	7-1-70	1400	S. Miller	7-1-70		
1	650	S B	S. Miller	7-3-70	650	S. Miller	7-3-70		
1	125	S B	S. Miller	7-6-70	125	S. Miller	7-6-70		
	6000								

Requisitioners Copy

...ty: Sue Miller, Ext. 459 ...en in.
Stockroom: Store in 4th floor storeroom
until called for.
CHARGE: Advertising Promotion Printing

REQUISITIONER

THE ABOVE ITEMS HAVE BEEN ORDERED FROM YOUR REQUISITION,
PLEASE NOTIFY THE PURCHASING DEPT. IMMEDIATELY IF THERE
ARE ANY ERRORS OR OMISSIONS.

telephone number of a supplier contact on any given purchase order. This simple idea also makes the expediter's job much easier. He can spend his time on productive follow-up efforts as he should, rather than looking up telephone numbers.

An attempt is made to reduce the number of back orders by stating that invoices are payable only upon completion of the order. When the supplier's credit department starts dunning for partial payment, it is politely informed that the order must be completed promptly and one invoice is preferred for the entire transaction. This transfers the supplier's credit department pressures to his own production facilities to finish the order so their accounts receivable can be kept more current.

Instructions to the supplier are included at the bottom left-hand corner. These instructions are generally standard, asking that the acceptance copy form be used to supply data requested and that the form be returned promptly. It also requests immediate notification of any delays, the use of the P.O. number on all packages and correspondence, and that all such correspondence be addressed to the purchasing manager.

The lower right-hand corner carries the signature of the authorized buyer and establishes, by its wording, that he is an agent for the company. This is legal wording to insure that any legal action resulting from the purchase order will be directed to the company rather than to the purchasing manager.

Before we leave the original copy of the purchase order, it is important to note the amount of space for writing the description of goods or services. Many of the forms used today are so loaded with instructions and EDP requirements that very little space is left in the description column.

ACCEPTANCE COPY

The acceptance copy is often referred to as the acknowledgement copy. Most suppliers are sales-minded and therefore inclined to accept an order. Since the name of this copy was changed from "acknowledgment" to "acceptance" a greater number of them have been returned. Often the acceptance copy is returned blank with the supplier's equivalent attached. Whenever this occurs, a close scrutiny of the supplier's reply is essential, because it could contain information making it a counteroffer. This could place the purchasing manager in the position of accepting changes or stopping the transaction at this point. It is preferable that the purchaser's acceptance copy be used.

The acceptance copy (Exhibit 4) is an exact copy of the original copy of the purchase order with the exception of the expediting data on the bottom. This portion pins the supplier down on correcting possible errors, explaining delays, and naming shipping methods and dates. It does not contain complicated "legal boiler plate" on the reverse side. The information requested is simple and reasonable, encouraging its use by the supplier.

The return of this copy by the supplier confirms that he received the purchase order, understands what is wanted, agrees to perform as requested unless otherwise noted, and furnishes the name and telephone number of his expediting contact. (Note: This could be a different person from the one the order was placed with.) Should trouble be encountered later in the process, all the information necessary to communicate effectively is at hand. This method of information gathering is known unofficially as preexpediting. All telephone orders are mailed as confirmed orders, but the acceptance copy is not generally used in these instances unless specifications are critical and written assurance of performance by the supplier is desired.

TRACING COPY

The tracing copy is used to expedite or follow up on the order. Since it is also an exact copy of the original, the supplier can use it if he cannot locate the original and desires to act without it.

The information requested on the lower left portion (Exhibit 4) is designed to show the promises made by the supplier on the acceptance copy and can be handwritten by the expediter. The lower right portion is designed to obtain updated information from the supplier.

This copy is easy to use and saves the time and expense of letter writing. It requires only folding and stuffing into a window envelope. Here again, simplicity and convenience engineered through proper design make this function an easy one to perform and encourage its use.

OFFICE COPY

The office copy serves as the purchasing department's transaction control. It is the home base for all information concerning each order. All communications pertaining to the transaction are routed to this copy by means of the purchase order number and attached to it. This copy is retained in a tub file, which is maintained by the expediter, during the active stage of the order. It is kept there until the receiving copy and invoice have been received, which signifies that the purchase order is ready to be closed.

Progress of a purchase order can be quickly checked at any time by reference to this file. When the transaction is complete the entire history remains attached to this copy (Exhibit 4), complete with the original requisition, the posted invoice data, the expediting notes, and all correspondence. There is an "invoice register" on the bottom for recording the invoice amount, number, date approved, and date forwarded to accounting for payment. It also serves as a defense against accidentally passing an invoice a second time and as proof that the invoice was passed for payment.

Reverse Side of Office Copy

The reverse side (Exhibit 4) contains expediting notes and contacts that have been made affecting the progress of the order. These entries are made primarily by the expediter who answers plant inquiries about the status of an order and handles communications with the supplier. In addition, this record offers an interesting insight into the quality of supplier performance. This copy and the other carbons that follow are used strictly for internal communications within the purchasing manager's plant. Confidential matter such as special instructions to receiving, charge account data for company cost records, and competing quotes appear on this and all succeeding copies. This permits everyone concerned to know promptly the details of what is taking place simply by distributing the order copies by interoffice messenger service on a daily basis.

Receiving Copy

The receiving copy is forwarded to the receiving department where it serves to notify the clerks as to what has been ordered so that they will be prepared to handle it upon arrival. Instructions are also included as to the disposition of the material upon arrival. There is a place at the bottom (Exhibit 4) for the receiving clerk to indicate that he has received the order and has notified the person concerned if it is a special order.

Reverse Side of Receiving Copy

The reverse side of this copy (Exhibit 4) is a receiving and issuing data record for special or partial orders. The receiving copy is forwarded to the expediter when complete. This lets him know that the transaction requires no further expediting and is ready for payment. It is attached to the office copy and held in the file until the invoice is received. When the invoice is received, it too is attached to the office and receiving copies and placed in the audit section of the file for final processing for payment and closeout of the transaction.

REQUISITIONER'S COPY

The requisitioner's copy (Exhibit 4) is a prompt notification to the requisitioner that his order has been placed. It enables him to see an actual copy of the purchase order that has been placed on his behalf and to check its accuracy early in the lead time period and also avoids duplicate requests. Should changes or corrections be required, they can take place promptly without adversely affecting delivery dates. This also eliminates the possibility of receiving an incorrect item and then having to return it and reorder the correct item. The saving in time and expense afforded by this procedure is again obvious: Requisitioners' follow-up calls and visits to the purchasing department are minimized. Most requisitioners file their copies for future reference. They become quite dependent upon them and will complain if they fail to receive them promptly.

EXPEDITER'S TICKLER FILE STUB

The expediter's tickler file stub (Exhibit 5) is filed according to promised delivery date or, in the absence of a delivery promise, two weeks from the date of the purchase order. This copy enables the expediter to review daily only those items due for review on that day without having to thumb through several hundred active orders looking for the ones needing attention. Again, much time is saved. If deliveries are running behind schedule, the expediting can be done sooner by following up in advance of promised delivery date and skipping a few days or a week ahead of the time specified in the file. This re-

Exhibit 5

Expediter's Tickler File Stub

TICKLER

No. 62082

The Evening Star Newspaper Co.

2ND & VIRGINIA AVE., S. E.
WASHINGTON, D. C.   20003

LINCOLN — 3-5000
GEN. 12 REV. 1-66

DATE _____ June 11, 1970

SHIP VIA	F.O.B.	DELIVERY DATE	TERMS - DISCOUNTED FROM RECEIVING DATE UNLESS OTHERWISE SPECIFIED.
Local Delivery	Delivered	July 9, 1970	Net 30 days

T O

A Lithograph Company
Main Street
U. S. A.

Attention: Mr. John Doe
(301) 555-1212

S H I P   T O

UNLESS OTHERWISE STATED IN ORDER,
SHIP TO ABOVE ADDRESS

ATTENTION PURCHASING

RECEIVING DEPT. 2nd FLOOR
STOCK CLERK

BILLS PAYABLE **ONLY** UPON COMPLETION OF ORDER

ITEM NO.	QUANTITY		UNIT	TOTAL

quires no changes in filing procedure. The stub serves only to identify orders that are due for checking on a given date.

This completes the analysis of each copy of the purchase order. Once the copies are separated and sent on their way, communications are so complete that rarely does the buyer or purchasing manager have to become involved again with a given order. Each step progresses automatically to an accurate and swift conclusion. This allows you more time to devote to other aspects of the purchasing function.

The purchase order system that has just been described is more efficient than casual, informal systems. Buyers using informal, undocumented systems seem to spend more of their time answering questions about goofed-up purchases and correcting errors than they do on necessary work. This, of course, creates a false workload condition, which leads to the creation of a larger staff than would be required to accomplish the job under a more formal system.

THE BLANKET PURCHASE ORDER

The use of individual purchase orders for restocking repetitively obtained supply items with nonvariable specifications seems cumbersome and unnecessary. The blanket order process is an excellent procedure for this type of situation, provided that the method of transmitting releases against the order doesn't involve typing correspondence. If written releases have to be mailed to the supplier, very little benefit will be derived from the blanket order process. A simple blanket order release form (Exhibit 6), designed for posting by hand, doubles as an individual transaction control and purchase history record for use by the purchasing department. The proper design of this system affords the administrative benefits claimed by such a procedure as systems contracting, but without the loss of direct transaction control in the purchasing department. Please note, however, that it is used on repetitively purchased supply items only.

The supply items are offered annually for bids. This preserves the values and fairness of competitive sourcing. Each successful bidder is then awarded a blanket order covering a twelve-month period. This is the only typed order that is issued; the releases against the order are placed by telephone.

The blanket order is written in contract language (Exhibit 7) that outlines the conditions under which it will operate. Pertinent information, such as price protection, delivery performance, billing procedure, and, of course, an escape clause covering poor quality or performance, is included.

The purchasing department maintains individual transaction control by using the blanket order release form (Exhibit 6). At the end of the contract period the release form serves as a complete historical record of such data as quantities, prices, freight costs, and frequency of purchases. This record is invaluable in analyzing costs and price trends as well as in budget forecasting.

The release form also gives the blanket purchase order number and the supplier and stock supply number. One form is used for each supply item. It is important to note that the form is designed to show the information in the same order as the "O.K. to pay" formula on the procedure flow chart (Exhibit 3). The first column shows the release number.

The order data section gives the original requirements—release date, quantity, and promised delivery date. The release number and order data are filled in by the buyer.

The receiving data section records actual performance—date received, received by, and quantity received. These items are filled in by the receiving clerk.

The cost data section shows the cost analysis broken down into unit price, extended total price, tax, freight, and total cost. This analysis is performed by the invoice auditor as part of his invoice checking process.

The invoice register section represents the O.K. to pay function and consists of the invoice date, invoice number, and date O.K.'d to pay. This section is also completed by the invoice auditor.

Exhibit 6
Blanket Order Release Form

BLANKET ORDER NO. _____

STOCK NO. _____

P.O.	ORDER DATA				RECEIVING DATA				COST DATA					INVOICE REGISTER		
REL. NO.	RELEASE DATE	ORDERED BY	QUANTITY	PROMISED DELIVERY DATE	DATE RECEIVED	RECEIVED BY	QUANTITY RECEIVED	UNIT PRICE	EXTENDED TOTAL	TAX	FREIGHT	TOTAL COST	INVOICE DATE	INVOICE NUMBER	DATE OK'D TO PAY

Exhibit 7
Blanket Purchase Order

Purchase Order

The Evening Star Newspaper Co.

No. 65805

2ND & VIRGINIA AVE., S. E.
WASHINGTON, D. C.   20003

DATE_____ May 10, 1970

BLANKET ORDER

TERMS - DISCOUNTED FROM RECEIVING DATE UNLESS OTHERWISE SPECIFIED.

SHIP VIA	F.O.B.	DELIVERY DATE
Most Economical Means	Delivered	SEE BELOW

TO
A Printing Company
Main Street
U. S. A.

ATTN: Mr. John Doe
555-1212

SHIP TO

UNLESS OTHERWISE STATED IN ORDER, SHIP TO ABOVE ADDRESS

ATTENTION PURCHASING
RECEIVING DEPT. 2nd FLOOR
STOCK CLERK

ITEM NO.	QUANTITY	BILLS PAYABLE **ONLY** UPON COMPLETION OF ORDER	UNIT	TOTAL
		The attached list of continuous data processing forms are to be supplied for a period of 12 months, beginning June 1, 1970. The specifications are to be equal to or better than the samples submitted with our bid invitation. No changes are to be made without advance permission of our Data Processing Manager. It is the responsibility of the Vendor to see that the above precautions are exercised so we may continue to have trouble-free operation of our Data Processing Equipment.		
		Numbered releases will be phoned in against this Blanket Order giving quantities and delivery required. We have the option of ordering either a 4 mo. or 8 mo. supply as our space permits using the rates quoted for each quantity. (See attached recap of quotes from your firm.)		
		The Vendor may stock pile form in quantities not greater than a 30 day average use item. (See average monthly use figures in our bid invitation.) A 30 day stock pile could be a valuable hedge against a panic order from us, and this amount would be redeemed by us in the event of forms change or discontinuance with no loss to the vendor.		
		Show Blanket Order Number and Release Number on all cartons, invoices, and statements.		
		We reserve the right to cancel this agreement in the event we experience unacceptable quality, service, or discontinuance of individual supply item.		

INSTRUCTIONS TO VENDOR

1. USE OUR ACCEPTANCE FORM.
2. SUPPLY DATA REQUESTED ON ACCEPTANCE COPY AND RETURN AT ONCE.
3. ADVISE IMMEDIATELY ANY DELAYS IN ORDER COMPLETION OR SHIPPING.
4. INVOICES, CORRESPONDENCE, AND SHIPPING CONTAINERS MUST SHOW OUR P.O. NO.
5. ADDRESS INVOICES AND CORRESPONDENCE TO PURCHASING OFFICER.

For The Evening Star Newspaper Company

BY_____

SAMPLER   PURCHASING OFFICER

For ease in filing and handling, as well as for protection during the year, each blanket order is kept fastened in an individual file folder along with a recap of the supply items with their prices and the appropriate release forms.

For those who do not have a basic formal purchase order system this may seem like a lot of detail. It is really quite simple; most of the actions are thought processes with very little manipulating required. The system is self-purging, because the transactions are closed with a minimum number of standardized documents retained. In every instance where time has been saved through proper design, control has also been gained by fixing and documenting responsibility and performance.

THE VALUE OF BLANKET PURCHASE ORDERS

Do you use blanket purchase orders in your purchasing operation? If not, why not? The antiblanket purchase order proponents contend that a blanket order system turns a purchasing manager into a routine purchasing clerk. This is not true—the use of blanket purchase orders will free you from an endless flow of paperwork and enable you to function as a purchasing manager should.

The blanket order, for example, offers the purchasing manager a way to reduce the paperwork required to process small dollar value purchase orders, which frequently account for 25 percent or more of the total dollars expended. You will have more time to negotiate larger and more important purchases. You can reduce standard, repetitive purchases to a minimum number with blanket orders and periodic controlled releases, and devote more time to creative aspects of purchasing, such as value analysis, market reviews, and price evaluation. In summary, one might say that the principal use for a blanket purchase order is to provide inexpensive procedures to obtain miscellaneous materials of low dollar volume. The time saved alone, while not usually calculated as a cost saving, can be worth many dollars.

How can you determine whether the blanket order system is good for your department? By viewing each purchase as part of a synchronized effort rather than as an isolated transaction, you can assemble clusters of requirements that are naturally grouped together. By analyzing previous purchases and patterns, you can group materials in various categories of importance. Two useful and general categories, for example, would be dollar volume and quantity of purchases. After compiling a list, you can then select those materials that most importantly affect your operations for immediate attention. In effect, you are systematically analyzing your needs.

Let's take a look at a simple case involving packaging materials. Statistical information on annual usage will identify the variety of materials, the different sizes of cartons, the units ordered according to size and kind, the ordering frequency of each, and the total dollars expended. From this data we can arrive at an estimated annual usage for the next twelve-month period, and prices can be negotiated on this basis.

Generally, a blanket purchase order needs merely to describe in general terms the provisions governing the agreement and to give a brief description of the materials covered. A blanket order is, therefore, a general agreement containing the ground rules without specifying any quantities. The material ultimately is ordered with individual releases containing exact information. Each release is identified by its own "dash" number (example: 1011–4) and can be a simple document printed in your own plant. However, some companies use a facsimile of their purchase order. It is important to note that some companies insist on actually forwarding the release to the supplier, while others merely use the release internally and telephone the order to the supplier.

Making use of this simple system accomplishes two major purposes: Quantity discounts are obtained, and overhead costs, such as clerical and buyer effort, are sharply reduced. A thorough review of your company's purchasing pattern may reveal many categories of materials that can logically be grouped together so that eventually many routine purchases can be eliminated. A little effort at mastering the mechanics can produce results that make interesting reading for every level of management.

The blanket purchase order does not depend on expensive or massive equipment, does not require a total upheaval of departmental or company paperwork flow, and does not demand any extra manpower or effort. On the contrary, it holds out the promise of just the opposite. It is a proven technique that can be used as a building block for better purchasing performance.

VALUE ANALYSIS PLUS STANDARDIZATION EQUALS COST REDUCTION

As the purchasing manager of a small company, your first thought after reading the title of this section probably is: "How can value analysis and standardization help me? Such programs are for the giants of industry." It simply isn't true. Value analysis and standardization can be practiced by a firm with a one-man purchasing operation as well as by a company with a hundred personnel involved in the purchasing function.

Before proceeding with the definition of value analysis and standardization, let us clarify one point that appears to be confusing to many people involved in purchasing. Some purchasing managers interpret value and value analysis as being identical. In the technical sense there is a great difference.

In a free enterprise system, with competition getting stronger daily, success in the business world hinges on continually offering the customer the best value for the price asked. Competition determines in what direction a company must go in setting the value content in order for a product or a service to be competitive with that offered by the competitors who supply the same wants and needs. This best value is determined by two considerations: performance and cost. Through the years, it has been generally recognized that a product must serve the customer's needs and wishes to the degree that he expects. That is, the product must have performance capability. Recently it has become clearer that the cost of producing must be such that the customer can buy the product at competitive prices.

This, then, introduces the concept of value, but it still doesn't tell us what value is. Value, like justice or liberty, is an abstract concept and has a variety of meanings. One common definition says that value is "the lowest price for a function or service, at the desired time and place, with the essential quality." Everything a person needs to know to contribute to higher value is included in this simple definition. We must have a product or process that functions, and it must be available when and where the customer requires it. Additionally, it must function with the customer's specified reliability. And, from a sound business viewpoint, most important is that all this be accomplished at the lowest price.

What is value analysis? Value analysis is the process of objectively studying every item purchased or manufactured in order to eliminate every cost factor that does not contribute to the functional value or usefulness of the item. It is a major responsibility of any purchasing manager in his search for profits. In addition, value analysis is an essential part of a standardization program, but it is not limited to things standardized. Many times, a standardization program results from a value analysis project. Conversely, a successful standardization program may well lead to the organization of a value analysis committee.

The foregoing is just one definition of value analysis, since no one has, as yet, presented a single definition that is acceptable to everyone. An attempt to be all-inclusive in a definition of value analysis would become so complex that it would scare away the very person whom the analysis would help the most.

You, as purchasing manager, are charged with the responsibility of obtaining maximum value for each dollar expended.

Indeed, the advent of a more competitive economy and the increasing complexity of modern business has made industry more anxious than ever to know it is getting its money's worth. Although skillful purchasing is necessary, it is not the complete answer. The modern approach to this responsibility is to go behind the requisition and the blueprint and seek the basic values in order to insure that the materials and services you purchase represent, in themselves, the maximum value in serving a purpose or meeting a need. Once you have determined the function of the item purchased, you are in an excellent position to offer sound recommendations for alternatives or substitutes that may substantially reduce costs while performing the required function.

No doubt, there are some purchasing executives who are reluctant to establish a value analysis program. They feel that their purchasing operation is not large enough or that their products are not complicated enough to afford such a program. These are excuses, not valid reasons. You may ask, "Why do you say we may have unnecessary costs in our products? What causes poor value?" Let us examine a few factors that cause unnecessary costs.

Lack of information. Whenever a decision is made, and we lack vital information, we invariably incur unnecessary costs. To keep abreast of our rapidly changing technology is a full-time task. There simply isn't enough time to wade through all the technical literature we receive. In addition, communications between departments can always be improved. Adequate information isn't always available at the point of decision making.

Decisions based on wrong beliefs. Each of us has ideas from time to time that are proved wrong.

Decisions based on habit. We are all creatures of habit; this in itself is good. If we had to reason out each of our actions, nothing would be accomplished. But when someone raises a question about a problem that demands an answer, if we answer by saying, "Let's do what we did last year," we are generating unnecessary cost.

Negative attitudes. Each of us, as he grows and gains experience, builds up in his mind a store of negative attitudes. Whenever we suffer a failure with a process or a product, this experience is filed away in our subconscious mind. Here again we are dealing with a human trait that has both good and bad features. This process makes it possible for some of us to reach a ripe old age; the difficulty arises when we allow negative attitudes to inject themselves in decision making on the job.

Reluctance to seek advice. Many purchasing executives seem to dislike admitting that they don't know something. In the medical profession it is common for a general practitioner to call in a specialist. The same thing should be done by the purchasing manager. He should call in a technical specialist or engineer if he has a problem.

In a small company a value analysis program is usually headed up by the purchasing manager. In any case, the head of the program must be a man who is profit-oriented, who knows his organization and his products, and who has the respect of the people with whom he deals so that they know he means business and believe that he will lead them down the right path.

What must be done to actually begin a value analysis program? It's really very simple. Select a relatively high-cost or high-volume item to analyze. It is, of course, to your advantage to select an item that you believe is costing more than it should. Apply the following tests for value:

1. Does it contribute value?
2. Is its cost proportionate to its usefulness?
3. Does it need all its features?
4. Is there anything better for the intended use?
5. Can a usable part be made by a lower-cost method?
6. Can a standard product be found which will be usable?
7. Is it made on proper tooling—considering quantities used?
8. Do material, reasonable overhead, and profit total its cost?

9. Will another dependable supplier provide it for less?
10. Is anyone else purchasing it for less?

That's it. A thorough study is almost certain to uncover potential savings. Incidentally, a value analysis program is workable even if you are a one-man department. In a small company the purchasing manager alone has the responsibility for obtaining full value in the transactions that he concludes. He alone must take the initiative to activate a value analysis program.

It has been a mystery, particularly to those who have used these techniques successfully, why value analysis and standardization have taken so long to become acceptable. The idea of having an organized program to seek the lowest cost to accomplish a function, and then to set forth the results of these analyses into a record for future use, is a natural for the purchasing manager. The most brutal answer is that purchasing people have sought to hide their lack of understanding by making such statements as "Value analysis and standardization are only for large companies," or "It's something the giants of industry use because they have plenty of money to throw around on so-called experts and fancy programs." It is more probable, however, that the foot-dragging is caused by general inertia and uncertainty as to just what these techniques are and how to use them. To many people, the terms value analysis and standardization are simply hazy words that have little actual meaning and are pigeonholed away as procedures that have no value to them. This is not so!

If we examine these terms more closely, we shall discover that most purchasing managers already have, to a limited degree, been using the techniques in their purchasing practices. All that is needed is a fuller understanding of how a more concentrated effort on just two steps would lead to more intelligent purchasing with resultant cost savings for their companies. These steps are (1) the actual analysis of material and equipment functions and of values, and (2) the agreement upon and setting up of clear purchasing standards.

As we said before, standardization is very closely related to value analysis. Generally, one of the first questions asked in the value analysis of a specific part is: "Can a standard part be used for the same purpose?" Standardization has to do with the study of materials, supplies, and equipment used, both for production and maintenance, in order to determine which quality is the best one to use for a particular job, and, after such a decision, to set up written descriptions or specifications of the desired quality for the future reference of all concerned.

The only justification for a standardization program in any company is savings. Some of the more commonly recognized cost-saving features that a good standardization program can provide are larger quantities of fewer items, more economical purchasing quantities, flexibility of inventory, a reduction of purchasing time, a reduction in obsolescence, the simplification of paperwork, and a reduction in the negotiation burden.

Regardless of how small your company may be, you can always use a standardization program to your advantage. Many current purchasing problems and pressures, such as misunderstandings between the purchasing manager and salesmen and the severity of emergencies and crash programs in purchasing departments, can be traced, in whole or in part, to the lack of an effective standardization program.

If you are a one-man purchasing operation, you are probably asking yourself, "How can I find the time for such a program?" Well, standardization doesn't take time from the busy purchasing manager; it conserves his time. Indeed, time is the most valuable thing we have today. When we use simple tools like standardization, we automatically make more time available for other duties. The basic objectives of a standardization program are to eliminate superfluous specifications, to develop the best part for a specific application, to increase usage effectiveness, to reduce costs, and to minimize the number of parts in inventory.

To start the program you should analyze the important

items that you purchase. You may purchase over 500 different items, but probably only 75 to 100 of these items represent over 50 percent of dollars expended. Make an analysis of your high-cost items to determine their status relative to standardization. You will find it very easy to pick out the ones that are "specials"—the ones that will show you the biggest savings if they are standardized. Next, you may have some items that are identical except for one point, such as color, grade, type, form, or material. Take a good look at these to see whether there isn't some way in which at least some of them could be combined for more advantageous purchasing and storing.

Standardization will save your company money. Just think of the money-saving possibilities in combining items whenever possible. There are fewer purchase orders to write, fewer items to carry in stock, and the advantages gained by quantity purchases. Purchasing a standard item right off the shelf is certainly a lot less costly than having to set up a machine and run the parts each time you place an order. And remember, standardization *will* work for a small company—the actual dollar savings may not be as dramatic, but the percentage will be there. Indeed, the small company may well find it means the difference between profit and loss. The guidelines in Exhibit 8 should help you establish an effective standardization program.

Remember—value analysis + standardization = cost reduction.

EDP IN PURCHASING*

You're never too small to have your own computer or at least the use of a computer. Smaller companies, like their larger counterparts, have stepped up their use of computers, and experts predict even greater use of EDP in the future. Accord-

* The author is deeply indebted to Martin Zwerling, Director, Data Center, Sinai Hospital, Inc., Baltimore, Md., for his assistance with this section on EDP in purchasing.

ing to a recent survey by the National Industrial Conference Board, four out of five small firms (the survey covered 160) reported that they own or lease EDP equipment. Many companies are currently enjoying the advantages of modern computer technology in areas directly related to the purchasing function. Competition in the computer industry is forcing prices down, and soon even more small companies will be able to enjoy the same benefits as larger companies through the use of minicomputers and low-cost time-sharing facilities.

Reluctance on the part of a purchasing manager to become part of the computer generation is no longer excusable or permissible. This section will serve to introduce you to the state of

Exhibit 8
Steps to Standardization

Start by looking over your stock of parts and maintenance items.

Take an inventory. Group items of similar type for the same use.

Analyze the cost of each item, and indicate the total inventory cost.

Next, discuss the possibility of using one major item for the same purpose.

Don't just discuss it in purchasing; discuss it with other departments.

Always have the facts and costs of major items available.

Review the possible reduction in inventory by better purchasing procedures.

Don't select minor items; use examples that will pay off.

Include a few smaller ones to dress up your presentation.

Zeal and enthusiasm for your convictions will go a long way in selling your plan.

After you have created some interest in this new manner of saving.

Take the time to point out that this is only the beginning of major savings.

Insist that you have the cooperation of everyone to put your plan across.

Once you have management convinced that you can save dollars, you are in.

Now, put your heart in your assignment, record your progress to back up your activities.

the art and to the promises of the future. We shall look into what EDP can do for purchasing and also review some of the pitfalls connected with it.

A New and Different Logic

The new computer environment requires a different kind of thinking. Some people have a natural aptitude and ability for this new logic. Others, who have been quite proficient in their work, may nevertheless find themselves subconsciously fighting computer systems and the inherent new concepts. The administration of a readily available programmers' aptitude test is an effective, efficient, and inexpensive method of selecting all levels of personnel who are certain to thrive in this new atmosphere. The traditional prerequisites of education and experience in a field may in themselves prove to be inadequate without the ability to understand computer logic. Aptitude testing will uncover the untapped potential of today's difficult labor market. Aptitude testing of existing personnel should not be overlooked as a means to recognize the up-and-coming purchasing managers of the computerized world of tomorrow.

The term "automation" is as relative today as it was years ago when the adding machine was considered to be an innovation compared with manual methods of computing prices and extensions of purchase transactions. Depending upon the size and special requirements of the purchasing function, any one of the various levels of automation available today may prove to be the most economical. A large company that purchases large quantities of relatively few items from a handful of suppliers will not require as elaborate a system as will a small company that purchases a variety of items in small quantities from numerous suppliers. Although the volume of purchases is an important deciding factor when evaluating an automated purchasing system, the complexity of the purchase transactions and the usefulness of the automatic byproducts (product analysis, supplier analysis reports, option to buy and cash flow reports, and so on) will dictate the level of automation best suited for your needs.

A carefully designed computer system can readily produce a great variety of features and reports, many of which may be considered byproducts of the basic purchase order system and are available at little additional cost. Two basic types of data input are required: (1) A listing of all suppliers, including name and address, identification code, and cash discount terms. (2) Purchase transaction information, including purchase order number, authorization codes, supplier number, product codes and prices, quantities and date received, invoice amount and invoice identification. Through computer programming, the following features and reports may be developed automatically from this data input.

- Automatic printing of purchase orders and *pro forma* receiving records.
- Automatic reporting of unauthorized purchase transactions.
- Automatic reporting of purchase transactions with new or unauthorized suppliers.
- Automatic reporting of total purchases of each item.
- Automatic reporting of supplier comparison and price fluctuation of each item.
- Automatic back order cancellation or reorder.
- Automatic updating, pricing, and reordering of inventory items.
- Automatic disbursement of checks including supplier's correct mailing address and remittance advice.
- Automatic deduction of proper cash discounts.
- Timely payment of supplier's invoices.
- Protection against duplicate invoice payment.
- Automatic charge-back invoicing.
- Automatic end-of-month accrual of items received but not paid and paid but not received.

- Automatic reconciliation of supplier's month-end statements.
- Timely end-of-month closing of books.
- Automatic printing of purchase journal, cash disbursement journal, accounts payable subledger, and prepaid lapsing schedules.
- Automatic posting to general ledger.
- Automatic record selection and testing for internal and independent audit.

Prior to the selection of a computer for purchasing and related accounting functions, the net worth of each of the features, benefits, and reports must be carefully evaluated. Cost comparisons of existing methods and alternatives must also be analyzed. Careful, professional planning will produce the most feasible computer applications at the most economical cost. In the smaller company, where the margin for error is decisive, the selection of the proper computer or computer service becomes extremely critical.

COMPUTER CONCEPTS AND SERVICES

New computer designs and packages are being introduced every day. The basic concepts may be described as the "batch" method and the "direct-access" method. In the batch technique, the data are usually collected on punched cards and held until needed to run computer reports, at which time the data must be sorted, batched, and balanced before processing and final printing. The direct-access concept allows all data to be available immediately upon inquiry through regular telephone lines via a terminal device to the computer. In this manner each user can communicate with the computer in a question-and-answer fashion.

A small, inexpensive computer will usually be classified as a batch type with a limited amount of area for the storage of data. In time-sharing, larger computers of the direct-access type are used. Some of the more popularly known computer concepts and services may be described as follows.

In-house batch computer. A small- or medium-size computer owned or leased by the user and operated by data processing personnel within the company.

In-house direct-access computer. A medium- or large-size computer programmed to perform many functions within the company. The larger systems allow the time-sharing concept to be used successfully within the parent company through the use of remote terminal devices operated by each of the user departments or branches.

In-house and computer leasing. A medium- or large-size computer programmed to perform the standard functions of a particular industry. This arrangement is popular in the banking industry where larger banks can afford to pioneer and maintain unique computer systems by receiving revenue from smaller banks for the use of the computer services. The computer configuration may be batch, direct-access, or a combination of both.

Outside service bureau. A medium- or large-size batch computer service available on a contract basis. Standard utility programs of a general business nature, such as payroll and accounts receivable, are offered to small companies that cannot justify and support their own computer installation. Charges are usually based upon the volume of transactions and the number of computer reports required.

Outside time-sharing. A large-size direct-access computer system servicing many users. Two-way remote terminal devices for sending and receiving data are placed on the customers' premises and connected to the central computer through the use of regular telephone lines. Charges are made on the basis of the actual duration of each telephone-connect time plus extra charges for special programming storage of data files and printing of reports.

Outside batch and time-sharing. A combination of service bureau batch processing and time-sharing direct-access processing, offering a variety of general and special services to users.

Specialized utility service. Large-scale outside computers of all types directed to meet the requirements of specialized industries. The high cost of research and development of unique computers and computer programs is shared by several users within each industry.

MINICOMPUTER VERSUS TIME-SHARING

Not too long ago time-sharing was reserved for engineering or research applications requiring high-speed complex mathematical computations that utilized only a small amount of input data. Many new time-sharing firms are now beginning to offer their products and services to the small business market; time-sharing is no longer experimental. Recent reports reflect an increase of computer sales to time-sharing firms that is rapidly approaching the 50 percent mark. Manufacturers are developing many new terminal devices to meet the requirements of the new time-sharing users. Time-sharing firms are busy developing new computer programs to meet small business needs, hoping to cultivate this vast new potential market. At the same time, computer manufacturers are developing low cost minicomputers, which are tailor-made to meet the budgetary requirements of the small company. The total effect is certain to benefit the smaller businessman, by providing the efficiencies and advantages of modern computers for as little as $200 to $500 per month.

The purchasing manager of the small company will, therefore, soon be faced with a choice between low-cost time-sharing and the minicomputer. Many elements must be carefully considered before a decision is reached. Assistance may be solicited from the time-sharing firms or computer manufacturers. Caution must be exercised, however, to avoid being influenced by facts and figures that are heavily sales-oriented. Selecting the proper computer or computer services requires a careful study of the applications to be automated. Maintaining an in-house computer is a great responsibility and a new experience to most small companies. Time-sharing proposals must be carefully examined with regard to the input and output speed of the terminal device, the amount of training required, prices and terms, documentation of procedures, degree of reliability, processing speed, charges for storage of data, computer language, file security, editing capabilities, and response time. In addition, the following questions should be answered.

- Which customer gets priority during peak load periods?
- What happens during scheduled or unscheduled computer maintenance time?
- Who has rightful ownership to specially written programs?
- Who is responsible for proper maintenance of data files?
- What protection is available against unauthorized use of confidential data?
- Can file changes be made without proper authorization?
- Who is responsible for verification of the input data?
- Will the computerized storage of data files and records meet the requirements of the regulatory agencies?
- In what form are records available for internal and independent audit?

As minicomputer manufacturers and time-sharing firms continue to compete for their fair share of the small business market, the purchasing manager will be required to strengthen his informational resources in order to make the proper decisions. A certain degree of actual exposure and knowledge of computer technology is necessary. Assistance from any experienced professionals within the company should be solicited. An alternative would be to enroll in an introductory course in basic EDP systems design and programming, usually offered at low cost by local colleges and computer manufacturers.

As a potential computer customer, you must first decide whether the applications to be computerized lend themselves to time-sharing. If not, is your company prepared to engage in a full-scale computer operation and all its ramifications? In either case, a prime consideration would be the availability of previously written computer programs, from either the time-sharing firm or the computer manufacturer, which can adequately meet the requirements of the applications to be automated. Another prime consideration is the amount of computer storage required to maintain the necessary data files of each application. Until such time that data storage prices come down, time-sharing firms must charge sizable fees for storage and file maintenance service. Computers with large storage areas or large secondary storage devices are at present expensive and therefore excluded from the "mini" classification. Most time-sharing firms charge for their services on the basis of the duration of the telephone connect-time plus many extras including data file and master file storage. More desirable would be time-sharing charges based on the volume of transactions similar to the manner in which service bureaus charge for their services.

The following checklists, which describe additional advantages of both time-sharing and in-house computers, provide a further basis for deciding which system is most practical for your needs.

TIME-SHARING ADVANTAGES

- Relatively small investment if service is to be discontinued.
- No investment in programmers or other professional computer personnel.
- No risk of computer obsolescence.
- Easy to train key personnel to operate conveniently placed terminal devices.
- No investment in pioneering or trial-and-error programming.

- Prestige of a computerized image created without computer overhead costs.
- No production peaks and valleys—computer used only when needed.
- No additional expenses for such items as computer operating space, storage space for supplies, nighttime operations, air conditioning, and security.

ADVANTAGES OF IN-HOUSE COMPUTERS

- Can customize programs to meet exacting requirements.
- Can readily modify or correct programs when necessary.
- More control over meeting deadlines and changing priorities.
- More accurate and timely printing of reports.
- Fewer processing delays.
- Faster recovery after unscheduled maintenance time.
- Less risk of unauthorized access to confidential information.
- No risk of increased time-sharing rates.
- No risk of time-sharing business failures.
- No risk of queuing caused by too many time-sharing users during peak periods.
- More control over misuse of data processing facilities.

What Can EDP Do for Purchasing?

Basically, EDP, automation, computerization, or whatever you prefer to call it adds a new, scientific dimension to purchasing. It expands, enormously, the amount of information the purchasing manager can use in buying, and the amount of helpful data he can use to back up his reports to management. Without question, an efficiently programmed EDP operation can help purchasing improve its effectiveness through better price performance, improved quality of purchased material, and increased reliability of deliveries. Furthermore, it can provide analytical reports covering a wide range of topics pertaining to purchasing.

Some of the reports produced by EDP for purchasing include:

- A daily receiving report to keep buyers up to date on deliveries.
- A daily edit report that indicates any corrections of prices, inventory data, or purchase order information.
- A daily receiving schedule that points up the price paid for each item and indicates any variance from previous prices.
- A weekly report that lists the stock number of each part, and indicates if the inventory is sufficient to satisfy outstanding production requirements.
- A monthly report that compares current prices with previously set prices.
- A monthly status report indicating quantity of each part in inventory, production requirements, open purchase orders, and expected delivery dates of each order for a period of six months.

One of the most serious problems confronting a purchasing manager is the daily review of extremely detailed reports. This daily chore robs you of a great deal of time. An efficient automated system handles the routine clerical aspects of this review and enables you to focus your attention on only the most important matters. You might say that it is a responsive system that enables you to make decisions and act on the basis of the latest available information.

The increasing complexity of today's business often forces the purchasing manager to be constantly "putting out fires." An efficient automated system offers tools that provide the purchasing manager with organized information, ready-reference data, and relief from clerical details. Such a system makes management by exception possible and results in improved overall performance.

In conclusion, remember, don't rush out and buy or lease a computer thinking that all of your problems will be solved immediately by pushing a button. Far from it. Computerized systems are not necessarily the answer to all of a purchasing manager's needs. Evaluate and investigate before automating. There are still many situations in purchasing where the addition of a few clerical personnel can provide the same basic information at a far lower cost than a sophisticated computerized system.

Make absolutely sure that you know what you want to do before you try to do it. Objectives take first priority. And another very important point—let it be a *user's* system rather than a *system's* system. Don't let a systems analyst tell you what you want—you tell him.

CENTRALIZED OR DECENTRALIZED PURCHASING?

If you ask ten purchasing people, "What is your opinion about the benefits of centralized purchasing?" you will probably receive ten different answers. No doubt some would say that there are no benefits. Centralized versus decentralized purchasing is almost as old an argument as whether to purchase ahead, or whether to indulge in reciprocity. The positions taken tend to be as extreme on this question as on the others—which seems rather pointless inasmuch as the best organization, in most companies, will generally include both centralized and decentralized purchasing. It is when multiplant operations must be reckoned with that opinions diverge most abruptly.

It is precisely because good points can be made for both concepts that intelligent purchasing managers should try to organize their department and train their personnel to keep and capitalize upon the *advantages* inherent in both, even though they may have to operate under one system only.

ADVANTAGES OF CENTRALIZED PURCHASING

Purchasing is inefficient if it is scattered or excessively decentralized. High costs result from lack of buying skill, numerous purchases in small quantities, poor financial control, overstocking, and delay in deliveries. Centralized purchasing, performed by a special department under a competent purchasing manager, achieves the following advantages:

- The purchasing manager and buyers can employ uniform policies and procedures consistently. And, of course, they can be held responsible for the results.
- It is possible to eliminate unnecessary variety in items purchased, thus reducing inventory investment. By establishing rational specifications, sources of supply can be expanded, and better quality can be obtained.
- Additional economies can be secured through the elimination of duplicate purchasing of small quantities, through central supervision over deliveries, and through such fiscal control of expenditures as central regulation of requisitions.
- It is possible to secure lower prices and establish good supplier relations (particularly on large orders providing for the aggregate requirements of the company) by utilizing effective negotiations, supplier competition, and quantity discounts.
- The time and quantity of purchases can be more effectively regulated through advance information on the trend of company sales and on inventory.
- Presumably, less manpower is needed, less paperwork is produced, and less time is consumed.
- Opportunities for value analysis are greater than under a decentralized operation, and, therefore, standardization can be carried out to the nth degree.
- Since the central purchasing department can always know precisely what is on hand, backlogs of obsolescent or surplus products, materials, or equipment will seldom accu-

mulate. If they do become burdensome, they can be sold off immediately from a central source.

- There is no duplication of facilities or responsibilities as is often the case in a decentralized operation.
- Because the department consists (or ought to consist) of professionals, the caliber of the staff should remain at a consistently high level; hence it should be no problem to select future leaders.

You should guard against excessive centralization. The degree of centralization should be greater if the materials and equipment of a multiplant company are fairly uniform or are identical. On the other hand, if the materials and equipment are highly diversified and the plants are scattered throughout a wide area, the attempt to purchase centrally from headquarters can lead to difficulty in achieving proper controls and obtaining the best service from suppliers.

CENTRAL CONTROL OF PURCHASING

Another method used by many companies is known as central control of purchasing. A corporate staff establishes policies and procedures and negotiates companywide contracts on high volume materials. Local branches of the company then place orders against standing or blanket orders issued from headquarters. In some instances the corporate staff negotiates a contract or agreement on an item and merely notifies the other plants of the details of the agreement via a purchasing newsletter. This method of purchasing is used when it has been determined that fully centralized control would be too costly because of freight costs or other reasons.

BENEFITS OF CENTRALIZATION FOR SUPPLIERS

Suppliers also gain from centralization of the purchasing function. Their salesmen need call only on one office rather than on several. Thus their sales costs are reduced and part of their savings may be passed along to you in the form of better prices. Additionally, the people they call on are usually better qualified and more knowledgeable about the companywide requirements for materials and equipment than are people in companies without a centralized purchasing operation.

Suppliers can expect fewer orders to be placed with them; however, those orders will be far larger in quantity and will require fewer invoices. Another benefit is that because central purchasing people are more knowledgeable, concepts such as standing or blanket order purchasing can be adopted by the central office, whereas in a decentralized operation, where they are unable to consolidate all orders, they could not even entertain the idea of introducing such advanced concepts.

DECENTRALIZED PURCHASING

Proponents of a decentralized purchasing operation offer convincing points for such a system.

- It is more flexible. This flexibility results from granting authority, along with responsibility, to individuals within the department. When spot decisions must be made, the man closest to the spot can make them.
- It reduces paperwork. You will recall that this benefit is also given by the exponents of centralized purchasing. However, the paperwork referred to here is not the paperwork involved in placing orders, but in correspondence with headquarters seeking approval, affirmation, or verification before a purchase order is actually placed.
- It promotes personal involvement in better purchasing. This argument is generally based on the assumption that because purchases are made directly by the user, he is more likely to insure that he receives the best materials at the best price, which can often result in savings.
- It is speedier. Single channel requisitioning can be swal-

lowed up in red tape that questions the quality, the quantity, or the prices of the materials on requisitions. Frequently, this results in costly delays and possible increases in prices that more than offset the savings realized when all purchase orders originate from a central purchasing department.

- It can result in substantial savings. Frequently, materials can be purchased locally at less cost, particularly those used by only one plant in a multiplant operation. This includes materials needed infrequently but urgently.
- It can result in extra services without extra expense. This is one of the strongest arguments made by the proponents of decentralized purchasing. Since local suppliers deal directly with the users, the goodwill, mutual dependence, and trust engendered by local purchasing cannot be duplicated when most purchases are made by headquarters purchasing.
- Mistakes are kept to a minimum. The proponents of decentralized purchasing believe that incomplete or inaccurate requisitions, are much more common in a centralized operation.

So there you have it: good points for centralized, central control of, and decentralized purchasing. As we said, it may well be that a mixture of the three techniques will best fit your company's needs.

It is important to note, however, that the totally decentralized system is less frequently used these days, as the advantages of the other two systems are becoming better known. The decentralized system used to be quite common, because it was thought that the engineering department could purchase equipment better than anyone else. The operations department thought that no one could buy and handle materials unless they were using them. As companies grew, management realized that centralized control would free such functions as engineering and operations of the responsibility for the purchase of materials. This gave them more time to devote to their own responsibilities—that of making engineering more productive and operations more profitable.

MANUAL FOR PURCHASING

Is there a need for a purchasing manual in your company? For a large company it is a must, but, as purchasing manager of a small company, you should make a study to determine whether a manual is desirable. Although a manual outlining policies and procedures can be very helpful, it can also be a source of irritation and conflict if it is poorly written. It is important to note that it must also have the support of top management to be effective.

At this point, there are two questions which need to be answered: (1) What are some of the reasons for having a purchasing manual? (2) Would a purchasing manual contribute to departmental efficiency? First, let's enumerate some of the reasons for having a manual. It can be used to define purchasing authority and procedures; clarify relationships with other departments and suppliers; develop improved policies and procedures; promote supplier understanding and cooperation; standardize and communicate approved practices; train new personnel and serve as a guide for others; provide standards for evaluating performance; and strengthen the purchasing function.

What about the second question? Will a manual contribute to departmental efficiency? The answer is yes. Having policies and procedures committed to writing is very valuable. Verbal instructions can be incomplete, inaccurate, and misunderstood. A manual helps you avoid these pitfalls. It also relieves you of the burden of unnecessary decision making. Most problems and decisions are repetitive; why should you go through the whole process of analysis repeatedly when the answers have once been found? With a clearly stated policy, you have only to recognize the problems, and the decision is automatic—the indicated course of action is clear. Moreover, when a policy is put into writing, it is likely to be carefully considered, with all its implications and with the overall interest of the company in mind.

There are many types of purchasing manuals. There are also different methods of organizing and communicating statements of purchasing policy and procedures. The method you choose will depend on the priority you give to the reasons already mentioned and the type of policy or manual selected for completion. The best way to develop a purchasing manual depends, of course, on your own particular situation—the kind and size of business you're engaged in. Another decision you will have to make is whether you want a single manual, which would include both policies and procedures, or two separate manuals—one for each. Most companies favor the single manual.

The actual writing of your manual should be carefully planned. You will need to establish a job plan, and, generally speaking, you will have three options open. The first is the gradual or evolutionary option—known to many as the 2- to 5-year plan. As problems develop, a related policy or procedure is drafted, discussed with appropriate personnel, and then issued. The advantages of this option are that it can be made part of the routine purchasing function, no extra manpower is required, and employee understanding and acceptance will usually be high. Quite often, however, circumstances will not permit this *gradual* option, which can be subject to frequent delays. This is where the second option—*the crash project*—comes in with top management approval and a high priority. Early completion is probable anywhere from a few days up to six months, depending upon the complexity. Employee acceptance and indoctrination is likely to come more slowly when the manual is issued. Somewhere between the gradual and the crash project options is the *scheduled program* option, having a definite plan of action, with the assignment of topics, review, and approval coordinated by the purchasing manager.

Repeated experience has proved that development of a manual for purchasing requires the same amount of project time (apart from routine day-to-day duties) as other types of manuals. For some unknown reason accountants seem to think that their manuals should take years to produce but that a purchasing manual should be completed in hours. In a small company, the job of writing a manual will more likely than not become the responsibility of the purchasing manager, if he has no one to whom he can delegate the work. There is little doubt, however, of the advantages of a team approach, with specific assignments being given to several individuals. The following work steps are commonly used for developing the total structure of a manual and also for drafting an individual policy or procedure. Only the scope of the project, participants, kinds of information, and final approval will be different.

First is the planning phase—to determine the purposes for which the manual is intended and the time schedule for completion. Second is the information phase—to collect the facts that will be useful or necessary to prepare the manual. Third is the draft phase—to discuss a preliminary draft, brainstorm the project, develop new ideas, and identify missing information. Fourth is the review and approval phase—where a consensus is obtained to assure a clear understanding and proper implementation.

Although this series of work steps may sound simple, collecting the necessary information may take considerable searching. No doubt you will find that a committee can seldom agree on how to write or how to edit. On the other hand, project members will come up with excellent new ideas and some valid criticisms. Their tough final review will result in a better manual.

Now, what should the manual contain? A representative manual would probably include:

I. A foreword by your president, executive vice-president, or general manager. This gives authority to the manual as a statement of policy.
II. Objectives of your purchasing department.
III. Scope and responsibilities.

IV. Chart of organization. A chart showing the position of the purchasing department in the company and the detailed organization of the department itself.

V. Limitations. A statement of requirements concerning the authorization to purchase, the final determination of quality, and a list of certain classifications of purchases that are exempted (for example: insurance, advertising, and rentals).

VI. Sources of supply. A statement of policies for selecting suppliers, such as dealing only with reliable suppliers, requirements of competitive bids, criteria used in evaluating sources, and reciprocity.

VII. Policies on making commitments. This section covers areas concerned with placing purchase orders. For example, all negotiations are to be conducted and concluded by the purchasing department; no commitments will be valid except as authorized by the purchasing manager. Conditions for acceptance of the supplier's sales contract forms would be included here.

VIII. Relations of purchasing with other departments. A statement of the importance of communications. For example, buyers are to be alert in passing on to interested personnel in other departments all potentially useful information gained through contacts with salesmen.

IX. Policy on personal purchases. It should be made clear whether the company allows employees to purchase items that are to be charged to the company and, if so, how the money is to be collected.

X. Plant visitations.

XI. Relations with suppliers. Policy on acceptance or nonacceptance of gifts or gratuities.

XII. Reports required.

These are just some of the topics that are pertinent to a purchasing manual; purchasing manuals should be designed to meet the needs of your own company. It is difficult to imagine that any purchasing manager would say that there is a good reason for not having a manual or, at the very least, a binder containing a compilation of purchasing procedures.

The steps presented are merely the first steps in the development of a manual. Remember, the development of readable, significant, and precise statements of purchasing policy and procedures requires organized effort, time, and persistence. There are many books available—even trade publications—that offer good examples. Today, as it will be in the future, a purchasing manual is recognized as a necessary part of a professionally managed purchasing office.

A COMPANY IS KNOWN BY ITS MANAGEMENT

In this particular section we shall assume that your department is not a one-man show but that you have several subordinates. Sometime ago, one of the speakers at an AMA seminar listed the features that employees said counted most in a job, together with an astonishing comparison between the way employees and their managers rated the importance of these features from the employees' point of view (1 = high; 10 = low):

Job Features	Employee Rating	Management Rating
Appreciation for good work	1	8
Feeling in on things	2	10
Help with personal problems	3	9
Job security	4	2
Good wages	5	1
Work that keeps you interested	6	5
Possibilities for promotion	7	3
Personal loyalty to the workers	8	6
Good working conditions	9	4
Tactful discipline	10	7

The order of items is not the most important feature of this list; it will vary from business to business. For example, whenever there is stable employment over a period of years, employees in that particular company will rate job security far down the list. The importance of these lists of needs that employees want us to fulfill is that most of them must be fulfilled by their immediate superior—in our case the purchasing manager.

The following ten sensible principles are noteworthy only because they are so old, so practical, and, unfortunately, so seldom practiced.

1. *Be humble with your power and treat each of your employees as an individual—respect his dignity.* Don't push him around. Convey to him that he is important and needed. When a man is made purchasing manager, he is given power over people. He can either swell up with that power or grow up with it. Too many swell up with it.

2. *Give him equality of opportunity and play fair in your promotional practices, work assignments, and overtime distribution.* In a Horatio Alger country such as ours, the conditions under which each person can advance as far as his talents and ambitions can lead must be carefully nurtured if we are to preserve individual initiative and competition—two of the foundations of our American "people's capitalism." A scrupulously fair upgrading system for hourly and nonexempt salaried employees is essential. Equally necessary are merit rating systems, formal development courses, and individually tailored self-development programs for potential purchasing managers.

3. *Let your subordinates know just what you expect of them; give them clear instructions; give them prompt decisions; and train them better.* If you want to learn something, ask each person reporting to you to write down his duties and responsibilities as he sees them. Then you write down their duties and responsibilities as you see them. Compare the two and be dismayed. That's why you should have a written job description for everyone.

Another big source of wasted effort is failure to take that extra minute to give clear and precise instructions. If you want to make assignments more efficiently, try these five simple steps: Plan the content of your assignment carefully; slow down in giving instructions; invite the subordinate to contribute; motivate him to do the assignment well; and invite questions on the assignment.

Finally, don't overmanage. Studies have shown that in general the best managers are those who allow employees maximum latitude. When you give a subordinate a job to do don't breathe down his neck. Don't be a "white-breasted or pin-striped oopster"—two of the most annoying birds in the business forest.

4. *Insist on high work standards; enforce firm, fair, uniform discipline.* Employees do their best work when they feel secure, and they feel most secure when they know what to expect from the boss. They are most productive when their boss demands their best performance and when he enforces strict but fair discipline.

5. *Let him know constantly where he stands and how he is doing.* The greatest crime in employer-employee relations—the one committed most often and extending clear up to the top of the managerial pyramid—is the failure to tell an employee how well or how poorly he is progressing. Most of us shrink from practicing this number one rule of management. In a survey conducted by a leading university, 75 percent of employees and managers reported that they were never or only occasionally told how they were progressing.

6. *Praise him publicly, rebuke him privately.*

7. *Tell him of changes in advance and explain the reasons why.* One of the most rewarding practices you can have is that of informing and conditioning employees of any major changes contemplated in your operations which may affect their habit patterns and peace of mind. You can use your company newspaper, group meetings, and memoranda to communicate.

8. *Satisfy his two-way right to know and to be heard.* As Claude A. Jessup, former president of Trailways Bus System puts it, "What people don't know can hurt everybody." Keep your employees informed about situations that they need to know about—situations that affect their jobs, their department, and the company. It has been proved that a fully informed employee is more productive and better able to understand the fairness and wisdom of management's daily decisions. Likewise, a well-informed employee develops a feeling of belong-

ing to the enterprise and is much less likely to hate the boss and damn the company.

9. *Be honest—go to bat for your men—don't pass the buck —keep your promises.* Check those off automatically as four common traits of your most popular and successful managers —no matter how tough and taciturn they may be otherwise.

10. *Give credit generously—praise the men and pass along the credit.* Mark well those three words: give credit generously. Ben Franklin once said, "You can do almost anything in this world that you want to do, if you don't personally try to get the credit for it." He then made this interesting comment: "On the other hand, it is almost impossible to avoid the credit yourself sooner or later when you don't seek it too anxiously." The people who work for a man do much more to make him successful than his boss does. By pushing the credit down to the people under you, you make them doubly anxious to pass the credit back to you, and this counterreaction sooner or later draws the attention of the top man to the big part that you played in the original ideas.

Well, there you have it—a blueprint for the daily handling of the very human individuals who work for you. There isn't one item in the ten that we do not have the power to give to our people, and, in giving, we earn the richly rewarding inner satisfaction of knowing that we are making democracy work at the workplace. The real trick is in making this pattern of conduct a way of life.

TRAINING ASSISTANTS

The purchasing manager must lay the groundwork for the development of competent assistants. You owe it to yourself to run an effective training and development program, because the purchasing department's performance is a measure of your own performance. Indeed, your professional progress will depend largely on your ability to build a capable staff and, finally, on the fact that you have a number two man ready to step into your shoes. A one-man operation is not efficient, for no single person can take care of all the details and responsibility in a department of any size and still do a good job at everything involved. The purchasing executive is only as good as his staff.

The pressure of daily duties makes it very difficult for purchasing managers to give adequate attention to the development of their associates. This, of course, is a serious problem, since the continuing strength of any business organization stems largely from the dynamic development of the talents and capabilities of its staff. Therefore, difficult as it may be, we must accomplish the job. The first step toward meeting this challenge is to hire people who not only are qualified and have the skills to do the job, but who also are motivated to do the job. The mere fact that a person may have one of these qualities but not the other is too often overlooked. Many who are not qualified would like to begin as president of the company. Then there are those who are qualified but do not want the job because of its relentless demands. Whenever possible try to promote personnel from within your company if there is a reasonable chance they will succeed. It is often more prudent to stay with a person whose strengths and weaknesses are known than it is to hire a stranger who shows a presentable résumé.

One very important point to remember is that most people welcome supervision and guidance. They appreciate a leader who gives them constructive criticism and helps them overcome their shortcomings. Too many purchasing managers assume that their assistants will resent such help; it is a key management responsibility to provide this kind of assistance to your personnel.

THE NEW EMPLOYEE

First we will discuss training the newly hired buyer. On-the-job training is the best teacher, but it is not enough to satisfy today's complex purchasing requirements. In addition to on-the-job training, the new buyer should be exposed to the seminar type of training program. Such a program may be conducted by your own personnel; however, it is strongly recommended that buyers be encouraged to attend annually at least one seminar or course in purchasing that is offered by a professional organization or other institution.

The new buyer should be given as much data as possible on your purchasing policies and procedures. Let him begin by reading a formal job description covering his particular job. A manual is an ideal method for presenting overall information. All forms used in your operations should be explained in the greatest detail.

If your purchasing department is large enough, one useful technique is job rotation. Through rotation, by commodity, the new buyer learns by actual experience the duties and responsibilities of several positions. In a small company the buyer may start immediately on an assignment, with you assisting him on the details. During his probationary period, as well as during the orientation meetings preceding it, the progress of his training must be closely monitored. This means preparing regular critiques in addition to asking the new buyer for his frank comments and questions.

THE CURRENT STAFF

What about the training and development of purchasing personnel already on the payroll? An excellent way to prepare buyers to accept greater responsibilities is to make them strictly accountable for their present duties and responsibilities. Don't attempt to recast everybody in your own mold. A purchasing manager should evaluate results, not the method used to achieve results. Many a capable buyer's potential has not been realized, because the purchasing manager concentrated on the man's methods of achievement rather than on his results. Specific goals should be established for a buyer, and the results measured against the goals. For example, such goals might be to reduce inventory costs by 10 percent, to reduce paperwork costs by using blanket orders, and to achieve savings of a specific dollar amount by using value analysis. Various alternative methods may be used to achieve these goals. The purchasing manager must not force a buyer to use a particular method—remember, it is the results that count, not the method.

There is quite a divergence of opinion concerning the relative effectiveness of learning by doing. To many people in management it is inconceivable that much can be learned merely by observing another person in action. Let us take a very simple example—learning to drive an automobile. To an experienced driver, the automobile is actually a part of him. He performs the necessary operations mechanically without consciously thinking about putting the key in the ignition, releasing the brake, setting the lever which puts the car in gear, turning the wheel, and so on. Yet, when that same man tries to teach his teen-age son how to drive, he finds that the only way to do it properly is to have his son sit behind the wheel and to instruct him while sitting next to him, observing what he does wrong and correcting his mistakes. The son will never learn to drive simply by sitting next to his father and observing him.

It is generally accepted today that people learn best by doing, and teachers teach best by observing students performing the function, correcting and encouraging them, and repeating the process until the students perform the task without need for correction. Thus the purchasing manager must teach, correct, and encourage his buyers.

Training, of course, is a continuing thing. There are new concepts in purchasing almost every day. You can learn these new concepts as well as gain new ideas by being an active member of a local purchasing association that is affiliated with the National Association of Purchasing Management and by attending seminars and courses of the kind offered by the American Management Association. Finally, remember that you can train and retrain, but effective follow-up on and evaluation of individual development is essential to a successful program.

JOB ANALYSIS, DESCRIPTIONS, AND EVALUATIONS

Job descriptions are less popular with purchasing managers than they are with those involved in general management. Yet they have many advantages for purchasing, and an analysis of your own job may help you to recognize them.

The term "job analysis" has long had two recognized meanings with correspondingly different objectives. One applies to the more or less superficial study of the work done and the conditions under which it is done in order to determine what the job actually is and what qualifications are required of an employee in order that he be able to do the work satisfactorily. The resulting information is summarized in a so-called job specification, which is used in selecting applicants for employment.

The objective in this case is to make it possible for the interviewer—in the case of the smaller company this would probably be the purchasing manager—to match intelligently an applicant's qualifications with the job requirements. It takes a lot of guesswork out of hiring and helps to eliminate labor turnover caused by misrepresentation or by lack of appreciation of the nature of the work and the conditions under which it has to be done. When help is scarce, applicants must be sold on the desirability of working for a particular company, and it is not unreasonable to expect that greater stress will be laid on the attractive features of the job than on the unattractive ones. If a new employee knows beforehand, however, what the drawbacks are, he will not be so disappointed and inclined to resign as he will be if he doesn't get the lowdown until after he has started work.

The second meaning of job analysis has as its purpose, not the preparation of a job specification for employment purposes, but the improvement of the method of doing the work. This involves not so much describing the work as dissecting it. The first step in this kind of analysis is to determine whether the work is really necessary; if it can be dispensed with, no more time need be spent on it. One test of essentiality is to ask what would happen if this particular job were discontinued. Elimination of unnecessary work on jobs is the first technical step in any improvement program.

Analysis is the breaking down of something into its parts for study. So it is with job analysis. It encompasses the thorough study of every single environmental factor affecting the employee and his performance, including not only the job requirements but the total physical and social environment in which he works. It is truly an investigating, fact-finding, and information-gathering process. Even a person who has worked in a job many years is likely to overlook many of the pertinent facts about the job. Experience and memory alone are not reliable. To analyze a job accurately requires, fundamentally, plenty of time. It is also essential that a guided outline be followed so that no factor will be overlooked, there will be on-the-spot observation of the employee in action, and interviews with the employee and his supervisor will be conducted.

Why should you analyze a job? Why do you need such complete and accurate information? It is the only way to prepare an accurate job description. It is the only basis for determining realistic qualification standards for securing the best employee. It is the only way to establish equitable wage rates, and it provides the basic information for employee training and supervision. The position analysis work sheet in Exhibit 9 illustrates The Macke Company's approach to the problem.

THE JOB DESCRIPTION

After you have collected complete and accurate information about the job in the job analysis process, you are ready to prepare the job description. A job description is important, be-

Exhibit 9

THE MACKE COMPANY
POSITION ANALYSIS WORK SHEET

Position Title: _____

Name of Incumbent Employee:

_____

To whom does this employee report?

_____
            Name   Title

Company _____ Branch _____Department_____

DUTIES AND RESPONSIBILITIES:

A. Briefly describe the usual and regular duties and responsibilities associ-
    ated with this position: _____
    _____
    _____
    _____

B. Describe any other duties and responsibilities not mentioned above. State
    frequency of occurrence and importance: _____
    _____
    _____
    _____

C. Supervision:

    1. Is this a bona fide supervisory position (right to hire/fire and/or
       recommend salary adjustments)? ____ Yes ____ No
       Describe supervisory responsibility: _____
       _____
       _____
       _____

    2. Supervision Received:
       Describe the level of supervision received; i.e. closely supervised,
       general supervision, free to make independent decisions, etc. _____
       _____
       _____
       _____

QUALIFICATIONS & REQUIREMENTS:

Briefly state minimum qualifications; i.e. education, experience, skills
(typing, shorthand, office machines), personal attributes such as speaking
ability, numerical facility, etc. Do not report the incumbent employee's
qualifications, but rather the minimum qualifications required of any employee to satisfactorily perform the duties of the position: _____
_____
_____

Have you discussed the above enumerated duties, responsibilities, and
qualifications with the incumbent employee? ____Yes ___No

_____   _____
        Date   Name and Title of person completing analysis

                        * * * * * *

Use the space below for any additional comments or information.

cause it provides the employee with a complete and clearcut picture of his responsibilities and duties, which is essential to good performance. It provides the immediate supervisor of the employee with the same information, which is also necessary for effective supervision. In a sense, it is a written contract between the employee and management. The job description provides the necessary information for the supervisor to prepare a breakdown of a job, showing the logical and sequential steps in performing that job. It is the basic document for employee training, performance standards, and work simplification for the elimination of wasted time and motion. Furthermore, the job description provides the essential information for job evaluation—the establishment of job grade levels and wage rates.

A note of caution is called for here. When you place Evelyn, Nena, Bill, and Pete in the same job, the different levels of performance of these employees will influence and often change the job description. For example, Evelyn and Nena may have considerable initiative and a spirit of cooperation, and often even volunteer for extra work. On the other hand, Bill and Pete may shun responsibilities, barely doing what they have to do. This, whether we like it or not, is prevalent throughout industry. Every organization should be flexible enough not only to permit growth and greater contributions to the establishment, but actually to encourage it. It is for this reason that all jobs should be carefully reviewed at least once each year, preferably twice a year, in order to keep the job descriptions up to date and to reward the outstanding employees.

Let us consider what the essentials of a good job description are. It should include an accurate job title—one that really is descriptive of the work—and the title of the job holder's immediate supervisor. A statement of the main objective of the job—for example, to provide for the efficient buying of all materials and supplies required by the company—and of the principal duties and responsibilities connected with the job should be clearly outlined. The common error here is to list only the duties or activities in the job and to fail to state the responsibilities. In determining responsibilities, consider the results expected. It is usually wise to include the following statement in a job description: "May be called upon, at times, to perform other related tasks not included in this description."

The job description should answer the question of how much authority the job holder will have. Some job descriptions lump duties, responsibilities, and authority into a single section. Usually, however, authority is treated in a separate section, which lists the executive powers that distinguish a job from all others. Frequently this section mentions specifically powers that are *not* granted to the jobholder, either because they are reserved to the next higher level of management or because they are assigned to someone else on the same level. For example, it might state: "The manager of purchasing shall not issue purchase orders for amounts in excess of $10,000 without the approval of the executive vice-president. The buyer of electronic supplies shall not have authority to issue purchase orders for MRO supplies except in an emergency."

Many companies feel that it is necessary to include a separate section on relationships. A job description should make clear how and in what situations the jobholder will work with others.

Be very careful to avoid meaningless generalities, such as "when needed" or "as appropriate," in the job description. Remember that the basic purpose of a job description is to convey specifically, clearly, simply, and understandably—*to the employee*—just what his job is.

Following are job descriptions for three different positions in purchasing: director of purchasing, assistant purchasing manager, and secretary to the purchasing manager. These are actual job descriptions used by three different companies.

TITLE: Director of Purchasing

BASIC FUNCTION:

Responsible to the executive vice-president for directing the purchasing activities of the company in accordance with established broad policies.

100

BASIC OBJECTIVE:

To secure for the company its requirements of raw materials, parts, equipment, and operating supplies at the lowest possible cost consistent with accepted standards for quality and service.

MAJOR DUTIES AND RESPONSIBILITIES:

1. Policies and Programs

   a. To recommend to the executive vice-president broad purchasing policies and programs in accordance with his forecast of economic and price trends in the domestic and foreign markets.

   b. To establish procedures for the control of purchases.

   c. To coordinate company specifications with those of the trade.

   d. To search for new materials of present or future interest to the company.

   e. To promote standardization of all purchases.

2. Organization

   a. To develop and maintain a purchasing organization that adequately meets the needs of the company.

   b. To approve position description of all immediate subordinates.

   c. To approve employment, promotion, change in compensation, or other employee movement in the organization.

3. Negotiations and Procurement

   To engage in negotiations for materials requiring commitments over extended periods.

4. Sources of Supply

   a. To engage in the development of additional or alternate sources of supply for important materials.

   b. To direct purchasing manager and assistant purchasing manager in similar activity.

   c. To promote, in collaboration with the engineering department, sources of supply for new or improved materials.

   d. To direct the maintenance of a list of acceptable suppliers, a record of purchases, and a record of prices and terms of purchase.

5. Relations with Suppliers

a. To promote and maintain good company relations with principal suppliers.

b. To direct purchasing manager and assistant purchasing manager in similar activity.

6. Contracts

To execute contractual agreements for the purchase of raw materials, purchased parts, equipment, and operating supplies, after view by the company's legal counsel.

7. Purchase Forecasts and Budgets

a. To prepare, in collaboration with the controller's department, purchase forecasts and expense budgets for approval and decision by the executive vice-president.

b. To submit such reports on the activities and future plans of the purchasing department as may be requested by executive vice-president.

c. To collaborate with controller's department in establishing purchase price standards.

d. To review with purchasing manager and assistant purchasing manager monthly material price variance statements submitted by the controller's department, and to recommend appropriate action.

LIMITS OF AUTHORITY:

1. To operate within established budget limits.
2. To implement major purchasing policy changes only after the approval of executive vice-president.
3. To execute contractual agreements for the purchase of raw materials, equipment, and operating supplies.
4. To execute company purchase orders for items of capital equipment in excess of $500 and upon receipt of proper authorizations.
5. To approve recommendations of purchasing manager concerning employment, promotion, or change in compensation of personnel in the department.
6. To approve expenses of purchasing manager and assistant purchasing manager.
7. To present papers and make speeches to outside groups regarding company activities and purchasing procedures only after obtaining approval of executive vice-president.

8. To limit his line authority to his immediate subordinates.

RELATIONS WITH OTHERS:

1. Directly responsible to the executive vice-president for the performance of the above duties.
2. Responsible for cooperating with all executives of the company in coordinating the activities of the purchasing department with other units of the company.

MEASUREMENT OF PERFORMANCE:

The performance of the director of purchasing will be measured by the effective degree with which he secures for the company its requirements of raw materials, purchase parts, equipment, and operating supplies at the lowest possible cost consistent with accepted standards for quality and service, and the degree to which he satisfies the executive vice-president with the performance of his duties.

TITLE: Assistant Purchasing Manager

BASIC FUNCTION:

Responsible to the director of purchasing for purchasing new materials and purchased parts used in the manufacture of the company's supply products.

BASIC OBJECTIVE:

To secure for the company its requirements of raw materials and parts used in the manufacture of supply products at the lowest possible cost consistent with accepted standards for quality and service, and in accordance with established policies and procedures.

MAJOR DUTIES AND RESPONSIBILITIES:

1. Purchasing
   a. To purchase those items and materials for which he is responsible.
   b. To negotiate claims resulting from damaged or defective merchandise received from vendors.

c. To negotiate the sale of scrap and surplus equipment only after approval of the director of purchasing.

2. Sources of Supply

a. To assist in the development of additional or alternate sources of supply.

b. To promote, in collaboration with the engineering department, sources of supply for new or improved materials.

c. To maintain a list of acceptable suppliers, a record of purchases, and a record of prices and terms of purchases.

3. Relations with Suppliers

To promote and maintain good company relations with suppliers.

4. Reports and Recommendations

a. To submit such reports as may be required by the director of purchasing on the activities for which he is responsible.

b. To recommend to the director of purchasing changes in policies, practices, and procedures.

LIMITS OF AUTHORITY:

To execute company purchase orders in accordance with established schedules.

RELATIONS WITH OTHERS:

1. Directly responsible to the director of purchasing for the performance of the above duties.
2. Responsible for collaborating with all departments of the company in order to effectively meet their requirements and to achieve his basic objectives.

MEASUREMENT OF PERFORMANCE:

The performance of the assistant purchasing manager will be measured by the effective degree with which he secures for the company its requirements of materials and parts used in the manufacture of supply products at the lowest cost consistent with accepted standards for quality and service, and the degree to which he satisfies the director of purchasing with the performance of his duties.

TITLE: Secretary to Purchasing Manager

Immediate Superior: purchasing manager

Handle all work to maintain the office of purchasing manager at all times, which consists of the following responsibilities:

1. Handle all correspondence for immediate superior which consists of pending, incoming, outgoing, teletypes, and telegrams.
2. Handle all dictation for immediate superior.
3. Maintain appointments and handle incoming and outgoing telephone calls as required.
4. Follow up and expedite correspondence for immediate superior each day. Follow-ups are pulled by the file clerk and put on secretary's desk.
5. Filing
   a. Maintain personal files as directed.
   b. Mark all correspondence for filing either in the follow-up file, firm file, or commodity file.
6. Handle correspondence and files required on special projects such as United Fund, NAPM, and other civic and charitable activities.
7. Process purchase orders, shipping releases, and change notices as required.
8. Make special reports as required by immediate superior.

EVALUATION

There are many purchasing managers who are convinced that there is no practicable performance-rating system that can be applied to the purchasing function. They are nevertheless aware of the desirability of having some form of measurement and have turned to an evaluation report. In most instances the evaluation report is developed by the personnel department. The reports used by The Macke Company in evaluating exempt and nonexempt personnel are included as Appendixes 1 and 2. This is a more formal approach and has worked very successfully for Macke. There are some who claim that an informal approach is more effective; however, the more formal approach is being used increasingly to lend some degree of uniformity to a plan to measure how well an employee is doing and to aid in his future development.

PROMOTION

As workloads increase or personnel leave, someone is usually promoted from within the company. How do you decide whom to promote? When a man receives a management promotion in a company, you may be sure his selection did not come about because the boss decided that Sid Burke was a good guy and deserved a promotion. There must be a need for such a promotion; a need backed by good, hard business logic. When that need is justified, management goes about the task of filling it; and it takes more than being just a good guy, or having long service with the company, to obtain this promotion. At least this is the way it should be.

The procedures for promoting a man may vary in detail from company to company, but, in general, they follow pretty much the way they do at the La Blanc Iron Works. The following story was related during a recent AMA workshop for chief purchasing executives.

Let's say that Director of Purchasing Gary Mader's department has increased its workload to a point where top management agrees that he needs another leader. His first step is to meet with Personnel Manager Roger McNeill. Together they go over all the personnel records of the eligible men. The personnel records at La Blanc Iron Works tell an important story. Not only do they record attendance, punctuality, special achievements, and additional courses of study, but, as a result of a review conducted every six months by management, each employee is graded on his job knowledge, efficiency, attitude, ability to properly carry out assignments, and relationships with fellow employees. These files are the starting point and provide information for the first screening process.

Length of service alone will not earn a promotion for a man, but, if all other things are equal, it will be the deciding factor. This is important because length of service helps to determine the extent of the prospect's dependability, loyalty, and stability. Next comes a conference to review intangibles which count so heavily in the final selection. Gary and Roger meet with Ed McCoy, purchasing manager, and Stan Wanger, manager of purchasing research. They study the screened candidates and discuss each man's leadership ability, his personality, his ability to get along with people, his ability to pass on instructions clearly and precisely, and whether he inspires confidence. His sense of fair play and the ability to use sound judgment are equally important.

Each candidate receives the same impartial consideration. No one is eliminated because of the personal feelings of those who help make the final selection. The chief aim of the discussion is the determination of the man's ability and his future potential to contribute to the success of the company's operations. If he qualifies in every respect and is considered superior to the other candidates, he is given the job. The new leader then embarks on a probationary period. This period may vary in duration according to the job requirements, but it is an important one for the successful candidate, since his performance is carefully checked and made part of his personnel records.

There is really no mystery about what it takes to move up the ladder. Logical, factual, and fair procedures encourage the employee to improve his abilities and build a performance record that will make him ready when the time comes.

COMMUNICATION

The new purchasing manager will soon find out that communication is one of purchasing's most pressing problem areas today. To perform effectively you must be able to make yourself understood by your associates, management, and supplier representatives.

Communication is the art of sharing ideas with others. Communication must be two-directional—you must be sure that the receiving mechanism is tuned in before you attempt to do any sending. Furthermore, you must constantly check to make sure that your messages are getting through. Poor communication or lack of communication often makes the difference between the failure and the success of a purchase, a sale, or a similar function. There is no limit to the ills and misfortunes that have plagued purchasing managers, or indeed mankind, because of improper communications. Basic problems become more difficult if necessary facts are not properly presented or understood. It is not always easy to present facts or ideas so that they are fully understood by other people.

A breakdown in communication can mean real trouble in purchasing. For example, the purchasing manager of a small company had the following experience as a result of a breakdown in communication between the supplier and himself. When partial shipments of a vital order began to arrive, the components were checked, and then rejected in wholesale proportions. Customer troubleshooters, teaming up with those from the supplier, studied the situation and pinpointed the problem. Made to print, the components would not pass the gauge. If not made to print, the components would pass. The supplier could have manufactured them either way. When they were received at the purchasing manager's plant, the components ran up against a serious difference in the inbound inspection procedures used by the supplier and the customer. What is more, the process sheet differed substantially with regard to the standards used by the customer and the supplier in testing. Far from being unique, this problem is typical of what can happen when customer-supplier communications fail. It happens far too often.

Another example of a costly breakdown in communication was between a purchasing manager and his quality control manager. The quality control manager didn't know that in changing the criterion from dimensional accuracy to a simulated performance range, he had changed a fixed-price contract into an open-ended, "best effort" merry-go-round. The quality control manager had communicated directly with the supplier without communicating with the purchasing manager. We need not elaborate on the results of such inadequacy in communication.

In a small company the purchasing manager can communicate directly with all personnel, but as the company grows the communications gap widens. How many times have you heard one of your associates say, "I get reams of information, but little that helps me in my job"? Yet, every bit of information withheld increases the risk of an inadequate, costly, or erroneous decision. Many of us think in terms of a single communication system, when in actuality there are a number of systems, each of which is beneficial in its own way. The following are the most frequently used communications systems.

> Formal: internal + external
> Informal: internal + external
> Work relationships: internal
> Grapevine: internal + external

Formal communication. The formal system is usually described on the organizational chart. It is the system charged with the responsibility of disseminating official information.

Informal communication. The informal system is normally used by clerical personnel in all areas of the company. It can be oral or written, and, if written, a memo is often used to transmit the message.

Work-relationship communication. The work-relationship system is a means of communicating that most of us use in our day-to-day jobs. If we each had to use formal communications, few of us would ever get our jobs done. The patterns are too complicated and change too often to plot an organization chart for the work-relationship system. It is not an ideal means of communication by any means. For example, a manager's secretary may wield tremendous influence in determining who is allowed to see him or whose work receives priority for his review.

Grapevine communication. Every company, small or large, has a grapevine. Some may call it a rumor mill. It is, without question, different from all other systems; however, it uses the informal system for communicating. It is very difficult to understand the grapevine system because it can, in fact, be used two ways: (1) to describe valid information, and (2) to describe inaccurate and injurious information. Both are transmitted rapidly—seemingly with the speed of light. Unfortunately, it is the second use that most of us are concerned about. To understand the grapevine system one must know something about human nature. All of us like to hear something that makes good sense. If the information we receive doesn't make what we think is good sense, we often invent additional data or interpret the fragmentary information so that it makes sense to *us*.

An effective purchasing manager will not issue partial information; his communications will make sense to all personnel. A few important questions to ask when communicating are: Is the language the simplest that can be used? How concise is the message? (The writer should strive for briefness.) Is there more than one interpretation that can be given to the message? Are there any misleading statements? Is the proper feeling generated? The writer should read his memo carefully to insure that he has not offended the reader through a poor choice of words—unless, of course, this is the purpose.

Today's purchasing manager has to analyze intelligently the tremendous wealth of information that is available to him, until he can define that which will assist him in obtaining results. He will remember that his superior wants to hear about cost reductions and schedules completed on time. He will sort carefully and selectively, looking for reports that will aid him in portraying and producing cost reductions while maintaining a respectable on-schedule condition. The revolution that has resulted from computerized information systems affords the purchasing manager a tremendously broad information base for better communication.

The old cliché, "What a man doesn't know won't hurt him," isn't true. Information freely given can make him more satisfied, more understanding, and more cooperative. It gives him recognition and an opportunity to be as helpful as possible. It is a fact that most executives do not spend as much time as they should communicating with their personnel. In the day-to-day rush of getting things done, they too often forget how important this part of their job really is. Nobody likes to feel that he doesn't really matter, that he isn't important enough to be informed or consulted about the situations taking place around him. An effective purchasing manager will communicate frankly with his personnel. He will talk about the job, the company, problems to be solved, ideas to be tested, anything that doesn't *have* to be kept secret. Remember, the more your personnel know about their jobs and the company, the more they can help—and the more interested they will be in doing so.

COMMUNICATION AND CHANGE

Good communication is invaluable when changes must be instituted in a company; it often means the difference between a smooth transition from old procedures to new ones, for example. This problem of resistance to change is dealt with in more detail in another section; however, it is appropriate to examine it briefly here. Resistance to change is universal and is applied to most things—food and clothes as well as procedures and policies. A mere suggestion of change is enough to cause a look of scorn to be cast upon the suggester. Why do people resist change? Very simply because change makes people uncomfortable. They develop a certain rhythm for doing things in the old way, and they don't want to see this rhythm broken.

Resistance varies in intensity among groups of workers. Unless it is checked in its early stages, worker resistance can be disastrous to the individual as well as to the system. It can result, to varying degrees, in a series of dangerous attitudes: personal frustration, a feeling of hopelessness, fatalistic acceptance of defeat, loss of vigor to fight, bitterness, and antagonism. There are some who say that age and length of service are correlated factors in a worker's resistance to change. Comprehensive studies by AMA have revealed that age and service factors have no adverse effect on employees' attitudes toward change. In fact, older workers tend to react more favorably to change than do their younger colleagues.

It is only logical to be aware of what people are like and why they resist change. Therefore, you should review personal characteristics and job aspects that contribute to resistance. Then narrow the list to specific items relevant to the personnel who will be encountered. Observe their psychological cycles or, if this isn't possible, chart your own. Your cycle will roughly parallel theirs, providing valuable insight to possible resistance areas. Be knowledgeable about departmental and company environment—its background, the organizational structure, problems and objectives, and peak workload periods. Become familiar with the lingo of your personnel. You'll seem less a stranger and more a friend who is there to help them. In short, study in depth the personnel with whom you deal.

When a change is installed, don't hinder the department's involvement in it. Resist the temptation to take over supervision of the change. Let go as soon as possible; remember, it's their system, not yours. However, you must follow up and establish adequate grievance procedures. Allow your personnel to have "ego involvement" with the change by giving credit and by allowing them to feel that many of the basic ideas were theirs.

Always remember one golden rule on the subject—good communication depends not on what you *tell* the other man, but on what he *accepts* of what you tell him. Today and every day, let each of us try to improve the art of communication so that our fellow workers, our associates, and others we contact fully understand us and we understand them. Let there be a complete meeting of the minds. In this small way we shall have added our contribution to improving the way in which we live and work with others.

COORDINATION WITH OTHER COMPANY FUNCTIONS

The purchasing manager must work well with other departments within his company. Purchasing is pretty much a focal point for everything that happens in a company; by necessity it crosses departmental lines. You must take the initiative in creating the right atmosphere in order to achieve active participation from and cooperation with other departments.

Purchasing is surrounded by interfacing functions, particularly engineering and manufacturing. One designs the product; the other manufactures it for the market. And since purchasing is the hub of the entire process, that process neither begins nor ends with the purchase itself. In defining these functional relationships and their shared responsibilities, the place of purchasing in the total business-management picture emerges as a vital profit center. A purchasing system, in other words, is dependent in its operation entirely on information flow, both from other functions of the company and from the external environment.

In your daily dealings with other departments you can contribute to the success of other department managers. But, your own success depends largely on how successful you are in gaining the complete cooperation of personnel in other departments. The effective purchasing manager is fully aware of the importance of good interdepartmental relations. You must be very careful to prevent disputes by defining departmental responsibilities clearly and also making every attempt to familiarize others with purchasing objectives, policies, and organization.

For example, coordination between purchasing and top management must be so close that any change of plans affecting the rate of production, or changes in the type or classes of commodities, will be brought to the attention of the purchasing manager well before the change is made. Failure to coordinate this important information with purchasing could well mean that insufficient raw materials would be in inventory, or, on the other hand, purchasing could be caught with an oversupply, which would also cause financial loss.

There must be close coordination with accounting to facilitate the completion of records for prompt payment to suppliers, to avoid all possible errors, and to take maximum advantage of all discounts.

Since the finance department provides the funds for purchases there must be close coordination there. As purchasing manager, unless you coordinate closely with finance, you may find that your hands are tied and you cannot take advantage of good offers.

Coordination between purchasing and engineering is chiefly concerned with matters of product design and specifications prior to actual production requirements. Engineering specifications may call for extremely close tolerances that place the requirement outside the scope of commercial standards, restrict the field of potential suppliers, increase costs, and increase the percentage of rejections. Therefore, a standardization program in most companies is conducted by purchasing, since it is an area where improvements can be made when purchasing and engineering closely coordinate their efforts. By doing so, there is a possibility of reducing the number of items carried in inventory and consolidating requirements, thus reducing investment.

It depends upon the product, of course, but in many cases it is up to engineering to handle the selection, development, and specifications of a product. As purchasing manager, you will select a reliable source of supply—indeed, it is your most important function in this regard. Engineering may sometimes assist in the investigation of potential sources of supply from a technical point of view. After a supplier has been selected and a purchase order has been issued, all changes and correspondence pertaining to the commitment must be transmitted through the purchasing manager.

You must realize that the effectiveness of your department is dependent, in large part, on the coordination of information between the other departments in your company as well as from external sources. You must also realize that it is important that it be coordinated in an organized and logical fashion. The following material is arranged to show what can be done to make coordination between purchasing and other departments most effective.

Purchasing's assistance to top management. Report activities clearly and currently by a formal and informal reporting system. Maintain records for top management control of commitments. Be constantly aware of top management orientation; that is, the overall company goal as distinguished from your departmental goal. Engender the confidence of management by performing well on the job.

Top management's assistance to purchasing. Carefully define the authority and responsibility of the purchasing department. Advise the purchasing manager of major plans well in advance. Allow purchasing to pay salaries sufficient to obtain and retain well-qualified personnel. Enforce the necessary coordination between purchasing and other departments.

Purchasing's assistance to accounting. Advise accounting of price changes in purchased material that may change the standard cost of a production operation. Advise accounting when inventories have depreciated in value, or when there is to be an unusually large expenditure. Always forward invoices to accounting promptly. (Invoices are often received by purchasing in a small company.) Consult with accounting before designing a new form related to accounting. Maintain a record of all commitments. Be sure that records are always accurate, to facilitate inventory pricing.

Accounting's assistance to purchasing. When requested, assist purchasing with financial evaluation of suppliers. Advise purchasing of account numbers and other data required. Minimize delays in payment of invoices. Provide special studies to facilitate value analysis. Provide purchasing with data on expenditures by category.

Purchasing's assistance to production. Provide required materials at the right time, in the right quantity, and at the right price.

Production's assistance to purchasing. Furnish requisitions to purchasing in ample time to avoid rush orders. Advise purchasing of changes in plans or designs. Furnish accurate information regarding requirements—don't overestimate in order to create a reserve stock. Maintain production control records and inventory records and make them available to purchasing. Cooperate in sampling new products and processes.

Purchasing's assistance to engineering. Furnish engineering with up-to-date catalogs. Circulate advertising matter to interested engineers. Encourage engineering participation in technical negotiations, value analysis, and standardization programs. Screen salesmen for engineering.

Engineering's assistance to purchasing. Consult with purchasing in setting specifications, and leave as much latitude as possible. Encourage covering all transactions in writing. Avoid rush orders. Allow as much lead time as possible.

Purchasing's assistance to receiving. Furnish copies of all purchase orders and "change orders" promptly. Avoid partial shipments whenever possible. Assist in planning for space requirements. Be certain that purchase order clearly states where materials are to be delivered.

Receiving's assistance to purchasing. Insure that all reports contain accurate information. Process receipt of orders promptly. In reporting damage, delay, shortage, and so on, establish, when possible, whether the fault is the carrier's or the supplier's. Notify requisitioner promptly on rush items. Maintain adequate and accurate file systems.

Some purchasing managers are always bewailing their lack of recognition from top management, but this negative approach does not get them anywhere. To gain recognition, the effective purchasing manager need only prove that he can do his part in coordinating his own efforts with those of others.

Accomplishment in this direction is shown by performance, not by talk.

REPORTS

There are some who will say that the purchasing manager of a small company need not make a report to management covering the activities of the purchasing department. But you cannot be too small an operation to make a report, even if you are a one-man department.

One of your prime responsibilities as purchasing manager is to keep top management informed about what is happening in your department as well as in the marketplace. Its unique relationship with suppliers makes purchasing one of the best informed sources of business intelligence in any company. Purchasing also has a responsibility to itself. It should make known its activities, its accomplishments, and its relationships both inside and outside the company.

What kind of reports should purchasing submit to management, and how frequently? Most purchasing managers submit periodic reports on their performance, either quarterly or annually. The annual report is preferable as a standard, with special reports being submitted, when necessary, throughout the year. The areas a report cover will, of course, depend on your type of business. However, there are certain types of reports that can be submitted regardless of the business in which you are engaged. One is the price performance of your department. How well are you purchasing in relation to the market? Another is a report covering savings achieved through negotiation. In any case, never fake a report on cost savings. Report only the true negotiated savings, not promotional deals offered to everyone. Of course, savings realized through such means as value analysis and standardization should be reported. A report on economic trends and market conditions would also be helpful.

In making a report, you can be sure that your manager

doesn't want a volume of words that say nothing. Nor does he want a report that is incomplete. The following guidelines may help. Tell him what happened. State in the opening paragraph what the report is in respect to; this will enable management to have a background for the details that follow. Write it from the reader's point of view and point out why it is of importance to him. Make it as brief as possible, giving all essential data in logical order; don't ramble. Tell what has happened since your last report, and explain the actions you have taken and why they were taken. Suggest what your objectives are for the future. Give deadline dates for completion of programs.

These points are equally effective for both oral and written reports. If the report is given orally, it is best to follow it up with a written memo containing the main points for future reference by your management. Remember, don't make a report for the sake of creating paperwork. There should be a sound, logical reason for every piece of paperwork created, circulated, or filed. If there isn't, it's a waste of time and money. By submitting reports to management on a regular basis, the purchasing manager will find that in keeping management informed he has also enhanced his own stature.

BUDGET

As purchasing manager for a small company it is very unlikely that you will be required, or indeed have the time, to prepare a detailed purchasing budget. A purchasing budget establishes the financial allowances for the purchase of materials required to operate. It contains estimated financial requirements for materials, tools, equipment, and so on and is influenced by price trends of the various items and, of course, by the financial position of the company. A well-designed purchasing budget insures the timely placement of purchase orders and the maintenance of adequate inventory to meet your requirements.

However, any purchasing manager worth his salt will maintain at least a simple departmental budget, which is primarily a means of accounting and administrative control. About a month or so prior to the beginning of a new fiscal year, you should estimate the cost of operating your department. Knowledge of the work to be done is a must. Included would be the labor cost of personnel required; proposed increases in salaries, postage, office supplies, purchasing books, and subscriptions; the cost of attending seminars on purchasing; travel expenses; dues for your membership in a purchasing association; and other similar expenses.

Where a detailed departmental budget is required, the accounting department must furnish you with the estimated fixed charges for your department. These would include items such as taxes, depreciation on office equipment, charges for service contracts on your office equipment, charges for holiday pay, and vacation and sick leave pay.

Establishing a departmental budget is fine, but if it is to be an effective operating tool, the purchasing manager must follow it closely. To maintain control, you must follow up the budget; that is, you must compare actual performance with budget estimates. You must analyze your budget periodically and take corrective action if deviations are discovered.

OBJECTIONS TO A BUDGET

There are many who object to a budget of any kind. Some of their objections and answers to those objections are discussed in the following paragraphs.

A budget is only an estimate and, as such, is often unreliable and quite possibly misleading. It is true that budgets are based on estimates. Their success, therefore, depends upon the thought put into the estimates. A budget should be used as a measuring stick rather than as a crutch or a dictum that is to be blindly followed.

A budget is complex and costly. As we said before, a budget should be as simple as you can possibly make it. Too much detail can be very expensive.

A budget is inflexible. They say that business conditions change rapidly today and the purchasing department that is bound by the red tape of a budget is apt to find itself unable to change rapidly enough to take advantage of changing conditions. This is not true. A budget *is* flexible. It should serve as a guide—not as a straitjacket. Remember, you must analyze it periodically.

A budget destroys initiative. They believe that a purchasing manager may become discouraged by having his departmental activities limited. This situation will not occur if, when presenting his estimates, the purchasing manager supports them with his plans. Then, when allotments are made, he can show conclusively that his ideas were sound.

In conclusion, the intangible effects of a budget are substantial. The thorough planning that goes into the preparation of a good, workable budget will earn the respect of top management for the purchasing manager.

RELATIONS WITH SUPPLIERS

Personnel in the purchasing department undoubtedly have more contacts with outside sources than all other personnel combined. This is particularly true of the purchasing manager of a small company. His efforts can help shape that familiar, though often mystifying, concept—the corporate image. What is the corporate image and how does it relate to the purchasing manager? For example, let's say that the purchasing manager prevents a salesman from seeing the production manager. Some people say that this is one of the cardinal sins of purchasing. It does not take an expert to see that this action may set off a chain of negative impressions.

The corporate image is simply the sum total of a salesman's experiences with and impressions of the purchasing manager, other purchasing personnel, and anyone else in the company with whom he may have contact. It is through you, the purchasing manager, that the salesman's sense of the corporate character grows. The salesman who calls on you evaluates the kind of treatment he receives. The personnel in his company judge your company by the manner in which your personnel conduct themselves in correspondence, over the telephone, and through occasional personal contact in meetings or plant visits. The image of the purchasing department is the image of the company. A good image makes the buying process easier; salesmen like to do business in a friendly, courteous atmosphere. Conversely, a good corporate image is even more important to your own sales force. In today's market, suppliers are also customers or potential customers. Salesmen appreciate an open hearing when they call, but if a company gains a poor reputation by the manner in which it does business, its representatives may be treated in a similar fashion when they try to sell their company's products.

There are many ways in which the purchasing department can improve its relations with suppliers. These are not difficult if they are done in a true spirit of cooperation. First and foremost is the policy of treating all suppliers fairly. There is no substitute for a reputation of giving equitable treatment to all —this means no favorites, no advance information on bids, no revealing of competitors' prices. Equal treatment for all suppliers is the best way to establish your company as one with which suppliers like to do business.

Second, in dealing with suppliers, you must make every attempt to keep your demands on the supplier reasonable. This is not to suggest that there won't be times when you must press for a seemingly impossible delivery date or try to negotiate concessions. However, there is no sense in applying pressure when it is not necessary or in blaming everything on the supplier when things go wrong. If another department is at fault, the purchasing manager should stand up to the requisitioner and protect the supplier.

Furthermore, it is often the small thing that can break a

reputation. It has been reported that some purchasing managers telephone collect when checking an order. This is obviously a petty practice and creates ill will far in excess of the money involved. If an order is worth checking, the phone call is part of the cost of doing business. On the other hand, if the order requires many telephone calls, the wrong supplier has been selected.

DEPENDABLE SOURCES OF SUPPLY

The first essential element of good purchasing is the establishment of dependable sources of supply. The purchasing manager might well be called the "business articulator," for it is he who searches the market and brings together in a working relationship those businesses that must serve one another in order to complete the productive process. When this interdependent organization is completed effectively, the productive process functions smoothly and economically. Needless changes in suppliers may break down this process. Just how close this organization of suppliers should be will depend on the nature and importance of the products they supply. If it is an important raw material, which forms the basis of the manufactured goods, the contact must be close and certain. If the product is both important and difficult to make to your requirements, the sources may be leased or held under a long-term contract. If the goods are furnished by a large number of suppliers, no close relationships can be established. If the product is a raw material produced throughout a wide area, it is probably sold through an organized market. In this case, purchases are frequently made in the market area nearest your place of business.

In any event, purchasing contacts with salesmen or brokers must be made at regular intervals. The manner in which you, the purchasing manager, conduct yourself in the course of these contacts will determine the prices, the goodwill established, and the future relationship between the businesses concerned.

Much of it is personal contact, and its importance cannot be overstressed.

A purchasing manager may buy from one to literally thousands of items from hundreds of suppliers. In the well-organized market of today this may appear to be an easy task, since catalogs, trade directories, sales people, and generally a product suppliers file (which gives a complete list of the suppliers dealing in a particular commodity) are available. Consequently, some purchasing managers are content to sit tight at their desks, treat visiting salesmen as intruders, and take an independent attitude.

If you are well organized, you will have an accredited list of suppliers that covers all items for which you are responsible. This list should be carefully assembled and usually requires extensive investigation and experience. It represents those who are in a position to supply what you want, in the quantities you demand, at responsible prices, and, of course, with guaranteed delivery when required. Revisions are constantly made to the supplier list as you determine new sources of supply. You must insure your company against all possible emergencies with respect to sources for the materials it requires. You must have ready sources to which you can turn should your company introduce new products or suddenly increase the demand for current materials.

One of the most serious errors you can make as purchasing manager is to assume that just because all companies are in business to sell products, the right products will be presented to you automatically. The amount of service, technical assistance, and quality control a purchasing manager can expect will be in direct relation to how profitable the supplier considers the buyer. It is understood that there may be brief periods of time when a supplier will accept an unprofitable relationship, but not indefinitely. The only good suppliers are those who can be your suppliers over a long period of time. Because purchasing is the usual contact between companies, it must create the conditions for a strong internal-external relationship. Such a relationship is based on certain expectations on the part of both the purchasing manager and the salesman.

The following list contains some important points that the purchasing manager should expect from the salesman and his company:

- Honesty and fairness in all negotiations.
- Accurate delivery promises.
- Ideas that will lower costs.
- Quality products.
- A sound financial base.
- Competitive prices.
- Constant research for better products.

On the other side of the ledger the salesman should expect the following from the purchasing manager:

- Honesty and fairness in all negotiations.
- Accurate specifications.
- Realistic delivery requirements.
- Opportunity to realize a reasonable profit.
- Nondisclosure of prices.
- Prompt reception when making calls.
- Reasons why he did not receive an order.

Evaluation of suppliers can be reduced only partially to statistics. Determining the quality of either a new or an old supplier is certainly one of the justifications for a purchasing manager. You are the one who has to make a judgment of the human element that makes the real difference in the relationship between yourself and the salesman.

An examination of all the techniques that have been listed for evaluation of a supplier indicates that they all relate to an estimate of credibility and probability that things will happen just as someone said they would. Statistical evaluation is useful for keeping score on delivery promises, product rejections, and similar yes-or-no, good-or-bad determinations. However, if you are not willing to develop the experience and judgment to weigh these possibilities and probabilities, you are definitely in the wrong line of work. For instance, one good idea from a supplier can justify a sizable number of late deliveries. Such factors as these must be balanced. Statistical evaluations can be useful only if they are not used as a crutch or used to avoid making a tough decision.

Potential Problems in Supplier Selection

Even if you succeed in getting suppliers who offer outstanding quality, delivery, and service at the lowest possible price, your selection of sources will not always satisfy everyone in your company. In many cases there are strong forces pushing business toward suppliers who do not necessarily measure up to these basic but tough economic criteria. Sometimes the environment in which you and your company operate influences the selection of suppliers. Relations with customers, top executives within a company, and the community in which a company operates may dictate the selection of suppliers on other than strictly economic terms.

Reciprocity

You will probably agree that a business grows by retaining its present customers and making every attempt to secure new ones. Therefore, if a supplier has proved to be reliable, if you believe he has a sincere desire to give you his best service and quality, and if he has a competitive price, wouldn't you say he is at least even with his competitor? O.K., whom will you give the order to? Will reciprocity play a part? Will the choice be made because of "arm twisting" by management? Will you want to favor a certain supplier for good reason? Proponents of reciprocity maintain that it is simply an application of the golden rule: "Do unto your customers as you would have them do unto you." Actually, reciprocity is a vicious practice that saps the efficiency of the economy.

Within recent years the government has taken a tougher stand on reciprocity. Indeed, the Justice Department has an antireciprocity bill involving two main lines of attack. The first deals with illegal reciprocal dealings where a company has established a "systematic reciprocity program," then made explicit or implicit proposals to customers, and consumated the sales. The second course of attack is to move on a reciprocity program even before sales have been consumated where the government feels that companies involved have sufficient market power to enforce reciprocity agreements. The Justice Department lists three types of reciprocity practices. The first is coercive reciprocity, in which a company seeks to obtain business from an unwilling customer by threatening to withdraw its purchases. A second type involves reciprocal contracts entered into voluntarily. Both are clearly illegal, say the antitrusters, because they adversely affect competition by excluding others. A third type is tacit reciprocity in which companies voluntarily purchase from each other without any agreement to do so.

It is the third type of reciprocity that has raised a great deal of controversy in antitrust circles. Legal theorists are split on the legality of reciprocity that arises in the normal flow of trading. To date, the Justice Department seems to have taken a middle position in this controversy, maintaining that it is necessary to consider all the circumstances in a case of tacit practices. In the view of the Justice Department, weight should be given to such factors as the volume of buying and selling, the respective size of the companies, and the opportunities that may be present to invite coercion.

In general, the Justice Department absolves purchasing people of widespread complicity in reciprocal contracts. Indeed, reciprocity demands the suppression of the natural inclinations of purchasing personnel. A good purchasing manager will resist involvement in reciprocal trading, because his job requires decisions based on price, quality, and service.

Does reciprocity pay? The fact is that managers in many companies have never stopped to think about limiting reciprocity; they are convinced that reciprocity pays. They believe that their sales department should use every legal weapon at its disposal to boost volume. They reason that if the company has to purchase something in order to make a sale, what difference does it make as long as the company actually needs the item and does not have to pay the customer any more for it than it would have to pay some other supplier? If the reciprocal sales result in a direct increase in the cost of the purchased material, a reciprocity-minded management may still approve the arrangements as long as the revenue from the sale exceeds its total marginal cost (including higher purchase prices) by a reasonable margin. In practice, however, purchase costs are rarely raised directly in reciprocal sales. Defenders of reciprocity also point out that it may actually help to reduce sales costs and that salesmen do not have to pay as much attention to accounts obtained on a reciprocal basis. Why bother, they say, if the account is in the bag? If a company gets enough reciprocal business, it can get along with fewer salesmen.

The High Cost of Reciprocity

Although, this picture of profitable trade relations may seem realistic, it is totally false. Reciprocity is inherently unprofitable, and it is least profitable for the companies that are its most enthusiastic proponents. Reciprocity actually increases the purchasing costs for the following reasons.

1. Reciprocity weakens and sometimes even destroys supplier price competition. Suppliers who prefer to compete on every basis but price become even less inclined to lower quotations when they know that business goes not to the lowest bidder but to the customer who is willing to meet his competitors' bids.

2. Reciprocity permits inferior supplier performance. Most reciprocal deals will sour when one party is consistently late and delivers materials that turn out to be of very poor quality. But a customer can get away for years with quality and delivery performance that is just a little below average. Buyers will know that he is a customer and will make allowances.

3. Reciprocity promotes inferior purchasing. In a company deeply involved in reciprocity, the purchasing department inevitably becomes sales-oriented. The objective of driving the hardest bargain, which is in the company's overall best interests, is subordinated to the objective of maintaining good relations with suppliers, particularly if they are good customers.

If, as purchasing manager, you concentrate on purchasing and do not worry excessively about customer relations, you can almost always cut costs. If you are not too concerned about hurting the feelings of one supplier, and another supplier offers a better product and a lower price, you will buy from the second supplier. However, in spite of its high costs, few businessmen would deny that reciprocity is here to stay. It certainly cannot be legislated out of existence. The only way to eliminate all traces of reciprocity would be to prohibit companies from selling to their suppliers, a cure worse than the disease. Moreover, a few companies will always find that reciprocity is profitable, even after considering its costs. Other companies will continue to be convinced that reciprocity pays, simply because management is ignorant of its real cost.

In summary, the company that is relatively indifferent to reciprocity earns a slightly greater return on net worth than its reciprocity-minded competitor, and the difference may very well lie in superior purchasing and sales performance. For maximum efficiency, purchasing and sales must be kept strong and independent of each other. Of necessity, top management probably will always be oriented more toward sales than toward purchasing. Thus every organization has built-in pressures that serve to make purchasing sales-conscious. Only rarely is there danger that purchasing will concentrate so hard on its job that it will offend the customers. The real danger is that purchasing will become so sales-oriented that it will not concentrate on buying. This is best avoided in a company where purchasing is the equal of sales—equal in *fact*, not just on the organization chart.

VISITS TO THE SUPPLIER

A visit to a supplier's plant is not just a junket that gives the purchasing manager a break from his daily tasks. Every visit to a supplier's plant benefits the purchasing manager in several ways. It is a means of seeking information and, therefore, should be planned well in advance. You should make a list of what you are looking for. There can be no standard list for use with all suppliers; however, it is possible to generalize somewhat with respect to possible items on your list. Such a list might cover the following areas:

Facilities. Your inspection could include production equipment and plant layout as well as the receiving department where the supplier handles his incoming shipments. The shipping department where he prepares his own products for shipment, the internal materials-handling system, and his office facilities are all important.

Housekeeping. Take a close look at his plant maintenance and general cleanliness. These areas can provide useful clues as to the efficiency and steadiness of output which you may expect from a supplier.

Personnel. You will want to make a close observation of the degree and type of supervision and the status of morale of his employees, since it might bear on possible strikes as well as on the technical competence of his employees. You should pay particular attention to his relations with the union. If a supplier is having continuous labor problems, his ability to meet required delivery dates will be affected.

Procedures. Particular attention should be given to the

manner in which the supplier processes an order from the time it is received until the shipment leaves his plant.

Research and development. A look into the supplier's R&D department will offer an insight into his state-of-the-art developments. You can determine how many people are engaged in R&D work and thus gauge the supplier's commitment to future projects.

In addition, you will want to check on the financial stability of the supplier. A supplier who is financially stable is obviously a better risk than one who is operating from hand to mouth.

Please do not construe the foregoing to mean that you should visit each supplier's plant. There are practical factors limiting such visits. For example, it does not pay to visit a supplier of low-volume items of small dollar value, particularly if the items are readily available from several sources. Visits to a supplier's plant are definitely worthwhile, provided that such visits are not overdone. They must be carefully planned in advance and you must spell out what you are looking for. The expense incurred is small when compared with the return to your company.

NEGOTIATION

Funk and Wagnalls' definition of negotiation is: "A conference or discussion designed to produce an agreement." A leader at a recent AMA workshop said, "Negotiating is the art of achieving mutual advantages without arousing hostilities." Whatever your definition may be, you will probably agree that negotiation is an art, a science, and a skill. Defining negotiation is relatively simple compared with attaining the skill.

If you were to stop and think about it for a moment, you would no doubt conclude that our private enterprise system is built around the principal of competition. Success in business is assumed to follow an ability to offer better value than that of a competitor. Although competition can take many forms, such as. service, quality, R&D, and technical assistance, price competition still remains at the top of the list. Vigorous price competition is the prime characteristic of our free enterprise system.

A purchasing manager is continually faced with the determination of whether a price is right or whether there may be room for negotiation. No two suppliers are likely to produce an item under identical conditions. There will be differences in the equipment used; machine speeds may vary; processes may differ; and, of course, the labor force will not be the same. Even though all costs of material and labor may be identical, they may still quote different prices, depending on plant capacity, burden of distribution, selling expense, and profit. In the final analysis, *prices are set by people—not by methods.*

Through negotiation, a purchasing manager takes the initiative to improve his position in any given purchase. Without negotiation, he is merely accepting the best offer given him. To refrain from seeking better prices through negotiation is to make the assumption that quoted prices are right.

Negotiation isn't haggling, or table pounding, or horsetrading, but rather the application of facts, logic, and economic pressure in order to achieve improved value or cost reduction objectives. It begins where the quotation price leaves off.

In the face-to-face discussions of a negotiation session, the purchasing manager has the opportunity to evaluate the supplier's interpretation of specifications, quality requirements, delivery schedules, processes, and cost estimates. Such a session gives him the opportunity to bring to bear his knowledge of the product, its manufacture, its market, and its cost, all in an attempt to achieve the maximum value for his company.

There are many books and courses available on negotiation but I know of none that can *make* you a competent negotiator. Your ability to perform the function of a negotiator is dependent on your total experience—on your education, beliefs, knowledge, judgment, and understanding of human nature.

Even the foregoing do not insure success; you must do your homework, and you must have extensive and precise knowledge of the subjects being negotiated.

The primary objectives sought by purchasing managers are attained through competitive bidding, negotiation, and even flying by the seat of the pants. However, wherever applicable, negotiation can and will furnish the best results. You must plan ahead to be successful at the bargaining table. Never dive in cold. The following are some questions that you should be able to answer before sitting down at that table.

- What are my objectives?
- What is the supplier's position likely to be?
- What concessions am I willing to make?
- Who should be included in my negotiating team?
- What facts must be assembled in advance?
- Can the item be negotiated? Does the supplier agree?

It is important that you establish an agenda that spells out what subjects are to be discussed, who the participants will be, and what the time and location of the meeting are. Get your supplier to agree on this. Many people have found it advantageous to conduct a dry run before the actual negotiating session begins. You can rest assured that your supplier will pre-plan before appearing for the negotiating session.

Once the negotiation begins, establish your important issues immediately. And make sure to take the time to define all the requirements. Otherwise you may both wind up arguing about different points. There are certain other considerations in negotiating that you will do well to keep in mind.

- Avoid invective.
- Keep the discourse reasonable.
- Be courteous but firm.
- Avoid ultimatums.
- Use reciprocal concessions when you have to.
- Never be on the defensive.
- Once you've made a point, stop talking.

The Negotiating Team

Besides other people in purchasing, who else can be helpful in the negotiations? Engineering, manufacturing, accounting, marketing, others? Be sure to use their talents. Who will be the chief negotiator? Generally, he will be the purchasing manager. Others should listen and take part when called upon, but only one person should commit the company or make concessions. Brief your team on all the facts and agree on areas of flexibility.

Other Considerations

Be certain that you are negotiating with those who can make decisions. It is absolutely useless to have discussions with people who have to refer every point back to the home office. In this regard, you will find that practically every salesman will claim he has the authority to negotiate—be sure!

Above all else, be a good listener. Explain your position briefly, then let the supplier do most of the talking. He may make concessions he never intended to make. Remember, however, you must guide the negotiations—don't lose control. Don't tip your hand too early. Withhold something for later concessions in return for a desired point. Negotiate for the major objectives, the long pull. Proceed from your strong points, but keep a line of retreat open. You are not trying to win a debating contest; you are trying to negotiate the best deal for your company.

Universally there is a disparity between what the purchasing manager believes he accomplishes through negotiation and what he actually does accomplish. An excellent tool for measuring your true accomplishments is a sound cost reduction program. At The Macke Company we have found a documented purchasing savings report (Exhibit 10) to be of immense value in this area. The following information about the report accompanies it and explains the procedure for completing the form:

PURCHASING SAVINGS REPORT

The purpose of the purchasing savings report is to assure the dissemination of data regarding the pricing policies of suppliers, so that other elements of the company can take advantage of favorable pricing as it applies to their particular operations.

This form [Exhibit 10] will be used to report all savings accrued through negotiations with present suppliers or a change of suppliers. When a change in the price of an item is arranged which results in a savings, the person making the change will complete the form and forward it through the regional manager to corporate purchasing. The corporate purchasing department will coordinate the further dissemination of the information.

Exhibit 10

THE MACKE COMPANY
PURCHASING SAVINGS REPORT

(1)   (2)

MACKE LOCATION   Lynchburg, Virginia   DATE   7/15/70

BUYER   (3)   Robert Miller

1. Item Purchased

   (4)   Widget, Brass

2. Old Supplier

   (5)   Smith Company

3. New Supplier

   (6)   Jones Company

4. Former Price (Specify whether each, dozen, case, etc.)

   (7)   .55 each

5. New Price

   (8)   .48 each

6. Estimated Annual Usage

   (9)   100,000

7. Estimated Annual Savings

   (10) $7,000.00

NOTE: (A) Once a saving has been reported, it is not necessary to report the same item again unless additional savings develop.

      (B) Always send one copy of this report to the Director of Purchasing at Corporate Headquarters.

Macke Form P-103

The form will be completed as follows: [These procedures are referenced to the form by number; that is, procedure one is identified on the form as (1).]

1. Enter location where savings were made.
2. Enter date of report.
3. Enter name of person who initiated the savings.
4. Enter description of item from which savings resulted.
5. If savings resulted from a change in supplier, enter old supplier's name. If savings resulted from negotiations with present supplier, enter present supplier's name.
6. Enter new supplier's name, or leave blank if savings resulted from negotiations with present supplier.
7. Enter old price.
8. Enter new price.
9. Enter estimate of the amount of this item that will be used in one year.
10. Enter estimated savings for the year. To compute estimated savings subtract new price from old price and multiply the remainder by the estimated amount to be used.

Only one copy of this report is required by headquarters; however, you may make as many additional copies as desired for your own use.

In summation, when you are negotiating prices you should recognize that quotations are essentially estimates that reflect, at best, past experiences. In negotiating, then, you should seek, not only to ascertain the objectivity of this past experience, but also to gain some understanding of what the future experience with the supplier will be during the purchasing under consideration. As does value analysis, negotiation digs beneath the surface concepts and rejects the assumption that competitive bidding automatically achieves these objectives for the purchasing manager. Negotiation is in no way contradictory to competitive bidding; it is merely a supplemental tool. Quotations are still solicited from reliable suppliers, but the quote is an initial step rather than a terminal one.

In the final analysis, your management is interested in profit contribution. Successful negotiations result in cost reduction, thus they are a contribution to profit. Materials costs represent the largest percentage of total product cost in industry today. Negotiation is certainly one of the keys to effective purchasing. It is a never ending task. The effectiveness with which it is used distinguishes a real purchasing manager from a person who is called purchasing manager but who is, in reality, an order placer.

DISCOUNTS

Webster's defines "discount" as "a reduction made from the gross amount or value of something." Anyone who has been appointed purchasing manager of his firm knows enough about discounts to know that there is much more to discounts than is covered in such a simple statement as the one just quoted. You may well run into any one of many types of discounts as purchasing manager, and you should be familiar with them. To name a few, there are cash discounts, quantity discounts, cumulative discounts, trade discounts, and prepayment discounts. At this point let's review each of these and the circumstances under which they are used.

Cash discount. A cash discount is not a price concession given by the supplier; it is simply an inducement for prompt payment of invoices. It is earned when payment is made in accordance with stipulated terms. Almost all suppliers offer a cash discount; however, the terms are not all standard. They will vary to some extent, the most common being 2 percent–10 days, net 30 days. This normally means that if payment is made within 10 days of the date of receipt of material or invoice (whichever is the later event), you may deduct 2 percent from the amount on the face of the invoice. Obviously, you must deduct the discount from the total amount for the material, not including any sales tax. Such terms as "prompt" or "net cash" are indefinite and should be avoided. Other cash discount terms are—

2 percent–10 days, E.O.M.—2 percent may be deducted if

payment is made by the 10th of the month following the month the invoice was issued.

2 percent–10th and 25th–2 percent may be deducted if payment is made on invoices dated between the 1st and 15th by the 25th of the month and invoices dated between the 15th and 30th by the 10th of the following month.

Net 30 days–the entire invoice must be paid within 30 days from date of invoice.

Net 10th proximo–full payment of invoice must be paid by the 10th of the month following the month of the date of the invoice.

Quantity discount. Quantity discounts are granted for purchasing in specific quantities and may vary widely in proportion to the amount purchased. From the purchasing manager's point of view, the question of quantity discounts is intimately connected with his company's policy regarding inventory. The lower unit cost realized by purchasing in quantity must be balanced against the extra investment and extra cost of carrying inventory over a longer period of time in order to determine whether the lower unit cost represents real savings. As purchasing manager of a small company, you should be very careful when you consider taking advantage of quantity discounts. You may find yourself in violation of legislation that prohibits price discrimination.

Cumulative discount. The cumulative discount is another type of quantity discount. It varies in proportion to the quantity purchased; however, rather than being computed on the basis of the size of the purchase order placed at any one time, it is based on the quantity purchased over a specified period of time. Cumulative discounts are commonly granted by a supplier as an incentive for continued patronage. The supplier granting a cumulative discount hopes that by doing so he will induce the purchasing manager to concentrate his purchases with a single source, the supplier, rather than scatter them over many sources.

There are those of you who will say that it is dangerous to

give your orders to one source. If this is dangerous, then giving your orders to many sources is uneconomical and costly. Furthermore, the supplier who receives a large portion of your business is more likely to give more careful attention to your requirements. Therefore, there are many advantages to concentrating your purchases with a limited number of suppliers, quite aside from the fact that you may obtain a larger discount by doing so.

Granted, the use of cumulative discounts is more applicable to some businesses than it is to others. For example, with perishable merchandise, the use of cumulative discounts provides an incentive for the purchasing manager to purchase in large quantities from one supplier, but at the same time it makes it unnecessary to risk the danger of deterioration in the quality of the product, which would occur if excessive quantities were purchased and inventoried at any one time.

Trade discount. The pricing system of many manufacturers is established on a graduated scale according to the manufacturer's classification of customers and without reference to the size of a specific purchase order. A trade discount usually represents the compensation of the purchasing manager who assumes certain distribution functions for the manufacturer. In other words, trade discounts are usually granted for the purpose of protecting a specific channel of distribution. It is normal practice for such a system to be linked with a policy of distribution through wholesalers, local dealers, or perhaps franchised outlets. Thus it makes possible an orderly chain of distribution by protecting specific territory rights, profit margins, and incentives.

There may be other bases of customer classification—for example, whether the product is for domestic resale, for fabrication, or for end-use. The price would depend, to a large extent, upon the classification in which your company is placed. Except in unusual circumstances, a purchasing manager will find it profitable to accept the established channel rather than to attempt to obtain undue trade discounts for direct purchases. At any rate, it is part of the purchasing manager's responsibility to see that his company is in the most favorable customer classification warranted by the circumstances.

Under the Robinson-Patman Act, the legal status of a trade discount is open to some doubt. If, however, it is used properly and in the absence of incriminating acts there should be no real question about it.

Prepayment discount. A prepayment discount is normally granted to fit a seasonal pattern. In recognizing the seasonal nature and/or frequent short cash position inherent in the nature of some businesses, prepayment or anticipation discounts and deferred terms are payment methods that extend credit.

Prepayment discount terms usually extend credit for 60, 90, or 120 days, allowing time for the purchasing manager to convert and sell the materials before the actual due date of the invoice, but also offering him the opportunity to earn a discount by making early payment. This type of discount is very similar to the normal discounts offered, with two exceptions: the discount rate reflects a more realistic interest rate of 6 to 9 percent per year, and the time allowance for payment is substantially longer. The following are a few examples of prepayment discount terms:

Net 10/60 extra. Under these terms invoices are due 70 days after the date of the invoice, and the purchasing manager is given the opportunity to prepay, discounting at the rate of 6 percent per annum. Payment before 10 days yields a 1 percent discount. Payment in 40 days entitles the purchasing manager of 1½ percent.

Net 90 days, ½ percent per month anticipation. Invoice is due for payment in 90 days and may be discounted ½ percent for each 30 days prepayment, permitting a maximum discount of 1½ percent.

Net 120 days, ½ percent per month anticipation. Invoice is due for payment in 120 days and may be discounted ½ percent for each 30 days prepayment, permitting a maximum discount of 2 percent.

The purchasing manager must be alert when negotiating discount terms if he is to realize maximum advantages for his company. Don't take what you read on a quotation at face value—negotiate! Many suppliers will quote identical prices and terms. When this occurs, the purchase order should be placed on the basis of quality and service. Usually one supplier will be preferable to the others when quotations are analyzed on the basis of quality and service.

ETHICS

The Random House Dictionary defines "ethics" as "the rules of conduct recognized in respect to a particular class of human actions or a particular group, culture." A purchasing manager in particular, and personnel involved in the purchasing function in general, are in exposed positions when it comes to the question of ethics. Purchasing, because it deals with outside sources and handles large sums of the company's money, is naturally liable to suspicion. There have been cases where a salesman, when he did not receive an order, insinuated that there was an agreement between the purchasing manager and his favorite supplier. Fortunately, purchasing is one of the most closely watched and audited departments of the company, and this is as it should be.

The purchasing manager not only must act ethically but also should avoid anything that even has the appearance of obliquity. A high ethical standard of conduct is essential, and there is none better than the *Principles and Standards of Purchasing Practice* advocated by the National Association of Purchasing Management, which represents purchasing personnel throughout the United States.

LOYALTY TO HIS COMPANY
JUSTICE TO THOSE WITH WHOM HE DEALS
FAITH IN HIS PROFESSION

From these principles are derived the NAPM standards of purchasing practice:

1. To consider, first, the interests of his company in all transactions and to carry out and believe in its established policies.
2. To be receptive to competent counsel from his colleagues and to be guided by such counsel without impairing the dignity and responsibility of his office.
3. To buy without prejudice, seeking to obtain the maximum ultimate value for each dollar of expenditure.
4. To strive consistently for knowledge of the materials and processes of manufacture, and to establish practical methods for the conduct of his office.
5. To subscribe to and work for honesty and truth in buying and selling, and to denounce all forms and manifestations of commercial bribery.
6. To accord a prompt and courteous reception, so far as conditions will permit, to all who call on a legitimate business mission.
7. To respect his obligations and to require that obligations to him and to his concern be respected, consistent with good business practice.
8. To avoid sharp practice.
9. To counsel and assist fellow purchasing agents in the performance of their duties, whenever occasion permits.
10. To cooperate with all organizations and individuals engaged in activities designed to enhance the development and standing of purchasing.

(Used with permission of the National Association of Purchasing Management, Inc.)

Whatever is done in purchasing not only must be right, it must also look right. Conducting business by the golden rule may be difficult at times, but it makes looking in the mirror more pleasant. Perhaps at this point it would be apropos to quote "The Goldman Rule": *Communicate unto the other guy that which you would want him to communicate unto you if your positions were reversed.* This rule was written by Aaron Goldman, president of The Macke Company and is on the desk of every Macke executive.

In a previous section we noted that it is the responsibility of purchasing to create a good corporate image. When purchasing is conducted on the principles just cited, it will greatly aid in the creation of such an image. We can spend millions of dollars for advertising in an attempt to create a good image, but it all can be ruined by a purchasing manager or others involved in the purchasing function if they are rude or abrasive in dealing with a supplier.

ETHICAL OBLIGATIONS

The purchasing manager's obligation to his company essentially consists in the responsibility for doing a complete and conscientious job. A few important points of ethics to consider are—

- Confidential information should not be given to a competitive supplier.
- If samples are requested and furnished, you should test them and the supplier should be notified of the test results.
- The personality factor should be eliminated when evaluating a supplier. A good purchasing manager will look at the matter objectively and purchase from a supplier, even though he dislikes the salesman, provided that he offers the best product at the lowest price.
- An effective purchasing manager will keep an open mind and be receptive to new ideas. He must not prejudge an item.

GIFTS AND ENTERTAINMENT

A few companies have adopted a rigid policy that the acceptance of gifts of any description is sufficient cause for immediate dismissal of the recipient. And they sometimes provide the additional stipulation that the supplier concerned will be rejected in favor of other sources when all other factors are comparable. However, most companies have a more lenient policy along the lines of discouraging the acceptance of gifts or special favors from suppliers that might create a feeling of obligation. Generally it is accepted practice to permit a salesman to buy a lunch or dinner; however, it is preferable that the purchasing manager also pick up the tab occasionally.

It is a fairly common practice for a supplier to distribute a gift to its customers during the Christmas season, and most often such a gift is given to a member of the purchasing staff because of its natural sales contact. In the majority of cases, this practice has no ulterior motive; it is a genuine expression of appreciation and goodwill, and is often prompted by a personal friendship that has developed in the course of business over a period of time. However, because of possible implications of commercial bribery, and on the grounds that such extra "sales expense" must eventually be reflected in the cost of material purchased, many purchasing managers have established a definite policy against the acceptance of such favors. Some companies absolutely forbid any gift acceptance by its employees. Others permit the acceptance of only such items as ball-point pens and calendars with the advertiser's name on them. These items are often used as "give aways" at conventions.

About six weeks prior to the Christmas season, The Macke Company sends a letter to all suppliers reminding them of our policy on gift acceptance. You may wish to use this letter as a guide, changing it to suit your specific requirements. The following material has been extracted from the letter:

To: *OUR VALUED SUPPLIERS*

I would like to deal frankly with a matter that I am sure has troubled all of us a little—the matter of gifts at the holiday season.

As a businessman I can certainly understand the appreciation for business that prompts a seller to send personal gifts to those individuals with whom he has dealings during the year. Increasingly, however, I have become concerned at the volume and elaborateness of what once started as a simple expression of holiday friendship.

The policy of our company is to do business with those companies whose products and services meet our requirements. Therefore, we urge that no gifts be presented to any of our employees. Your strict compliance with this request will be appreciated.

If, in the holiday spirit, you may wish to acknowledge your regard for The Macke Company or for some particular manager or employee, I suggest that you may want to make a contribution in the Macke name to your own favorite charity. I would like to stress again, however, that no such contributions are solicited or are required to reinforce your business relationships with our company.

Your high regard for us can be expressed by your strict compliance with the policy stated in this letter.

Sincerely,

SHARP PRACTICES

Item number 8 of NAPM's *Principles and Standards of Purchasing Practice* states that purchasing employees should "avoid sharp practice." The term sharp practice is probably best defined by some typical illustrations of evasion and indirect misrepresentation just short of actual fraud. They belong to the "green eyeshade boys" of years gone by when purchasing was concerned with the immediate transaction rather than a long-range program. Such practices are frowned upon today by purchasing managers themselves, because modern purchasing practices are based on mutual confidence and integrity.

No doubt you have heard of one or more of the following sharp practices: (1) Asking for more bids than necessary in the hope that a supplier will make an error in his estimate, which the purchasing manager can take advantage of. (2) Leaving copies of competitive suppliers' bids or price lists in open view while negotiating with a salesman, with full knowledge that the salesman can't help noticing them. (3) Discussing a proposed contract in terms of large quantities, encouraging the supplier to expect a large volume of business and to quote on a quantity basis, when in fact the actual requirement is in relatively small volume that would not legitimately qualify for quantity consideration.

These practices should not be confused with normal shrewd negotiation, which is expected of a good purchasing manager. Indeed, the efficient purchasing manager will make maximum use of his company's purchasing power.

THE OTHER SIDE OF THE COIN

Business ethics is not a one-way street. Occasionally, a purchasing manager is confronted with unethical sales practices, although such instances are no more representative of sales policy than are the cases of unethical purchasing. Among sharp practices in selling are such acts as collusion in bidding, restrictive conditions in specifications, sabotage of competitive products, and magnification of sample orders into excessive quantities. These can be avoided by the proper selection of suppliers, but often this is not done until after an unfortunate experience has indicated a disreputable supplier. More direct and aggressive action is called for as a corrective measure in dealing with some of these practices, such as in collusion in bidding.

The best defense against sharp selling practices is competent, objective purchasing, supported by the necessary follow-through and insistence on contract performance, acceptance testing, and so on. As you know, the purchase order itself constitutes a legally enforceable document. Any and all supplementary agreements, specifications, and special terms should likewise be reduced to writing, using care to see that no ambiguity exists in respect to what is expected of the supplier. Needless to say, reputable suppliers respect the purchasing manager who is alert, thorough, and conscientious in the conduct of his office, and they, in turn, reciprocate. Purchasing's opportunities for developing a good image are so frequent that its success in this area should be a measure of its performance evaluation.

LEGAL ASPECTS OF PURCHASING

According to an old maxim, "a little law is a dangerous thing." A reply to this might be, "no law is a worse thing." If a purchasing manager, with limited legal knowledge, regards himself as an authority on legal matters and considers attorneys unnecessary, his limited knowledge of the law will be particularly dangerous. Purchasing managers need to learn enough about contract law at least to know when professional legal advice is required.

All materials used by a company will be acquired by some form of contract. The contract may be oral or written. Certainly all materials of high dollar value should be acquired by using a purchase order, which is an agreement that can be legally enforced. Even an oral agreement is enforceable by legal proceedings. Indeed, contracts are concluded daily by a formal handshake, and integrity is expected of both parties. However, except in unusual circumstances, a written purchase order should be used for all purchases. The terms, conditions and specifications for materials will usually be of such detail that considerable care must be exercised to prevent misunderstandings. Legal problems do develop from simple misunderstandings, and this can become quite expensive.

A CONTRACT

A contract is an agreement, duly made, between two or more competent parties, to do or not to do a specific lawful thing for a consideration. The agreement is constituted first of an *offer*. There must be an offer and an acceptance to indicate agreement of both parties. The offer must be definite, must be communicated, and must express the intention of creating a legal obligation. If it is too vague to be enforceable by the courts, it is not an offer.

Once an offer is made, it remains in effect until it is terminated by: (1) revocation by the person or company making the offer; (2) lapse of a specified time or a reasonable time (depending upon the nature of the goods); (3) rejection by the person or company receiving the offer; (4) counteroffer by the person or company to whom the offer was made; or (5) illegality. The offer may also be withdrawn at any time before its acceptance.

The second part of the agreement is the *acceptance* by both parties. An acceptance must (1) be accepted by the person or company to whom the offer was made; (2) be a complete understanding of both parties as to the intention of the contract; (3) be absolute, unconditional, and identical with the offer; (4) indicate acceptance by word or action; and (5) be communicated.

It is important to note that if a sales order is sent in response to a purchase order, the sales order becomes a counteroffer. Unless exception is taken to the counteroffer, acceptance of the goods shipped becomes an acceptance of the counteroffer. A purchasing manager should be on guard for conflicting terms of any written offers or acceptances. Such conflicts may present his company with a legal problem.

Misrepresentation. As a general rule, if one party to a contract makes a statement of fact which is false, but he does so innocently without intending to deceive the other party, the contract will stand. However, if one party takes an unfair advantage of the other, the contract may be unenforceable. The contract can be voided if there is false representation or concealment of a present or past material act. The person making a false representation must know his representation is false and the misrepresentation must be made with the intention of influencing the other party to believe in it or to act upon it. Indeed, there can be a case of fraud if the foregoing conditions exist.

Words used in a contract need not be complicated. As a matter of fact, except in unusual cases, it is desirable to use the simplest and briefest wording possible—just make sure that the intent is clear.

According to the Uniform Commercial Code, Section 2–201, any contract for materials with a value of $500 or more must be in writing to be enforceable. However, there is an exception. Under the following special conditions, a contract in the amount of $500 or more may be enforceable even when not in writing: (1) The materials were manufactured especially for the purchaser and are not suitable for sale to others; (2) The party against whom enforcement is being sought agrees in court that a contract was made; or (3) the materials have been accepted and payment made.

You should keep these points of law in mind when making oral agreements. Simply to furnish the supplier with a purchase order number is not sufficient to make a contract. Generally speaking, it is best to follow up an oral agreement with a written purchase order or agreement.

Law of Agency

The purchasing manager for a small company may not fully realize what the legal ramifications of his title are or that under certain conditions he can be held liable for a contract. An *agent* (purchasing manager in this example) is a person authorized to act for another known as a principal (the company).

The authority of a purchasing manager is created by delegation. He has *actual or specific authority,* which creates an "agency" in the bylaws of the company. He also has *apparent authority.* Trade practice, the actual acts of a person, or the normal scope of activities encompassed by his title may give a person apparent authority to act for his principal.

In the absence of definite knowledge to the contrary, a supplier may assume that a purchasing manager has the same duties and limitations as purchasing managers in similar positions in the trade. Usually, a salesman only solicits orders. He normally cannot bind his principal by his representations or his acceptance of a purchase order. The purchase order must be approved by his home office before it is binding.

Ordinarily, the title "purchasing manager" indicates that the purchasing manager is acting (as an agent) for someone else and not in his own behalf. Therefore, practically all companies prefer to have their purchase orders bear the signature and *title* of the purchasing manager. In fact, legally, to make the company liable, purchase orders should be signed in one of the following manners.

XYZ COMPANY   XYZ COMPANY

By: _____ *or* By: _____
    Purchasing Manager   Authorized Signature

When a purchasing manager exceeds both his actual authority and his apparent authority, he is personally liable to the party with whom the contract was made, unless, of course, his principal later approves the contract or accepts benefits from it. When a purchasing manager exceeds his actual authority but not his apparent authority, the principal is bound by the purchasing manager's actions and the purchasing manager is personally liable to his principal. Keep in mind that a company or corporation is, in reality, a fictitious person—it can enter into a contract only through an agent, a living person.

LAW OF SALES

Unless otherwise stated in the contract, all transactions will have some type of warranty on the materials or services. The warranties may be express or implied.

Express warranty is any affirmation of fact or any promise by the seller relating to the materials, if the natural tendency of such affirmation or promise is to induce the purchase manager (or buyer) to purchase the materials and if the purchasing manager (or buyer) purchasing the materials is relying thereon.

Implied warranty is one deducible from conduct or circumstances or one implied in law from considerations of public policy, such as warranty of title. The contracting parties may expressly agree that one or more of the implied warranties do not apply to their contract. In the case of warranty of title, the seller implicitly warrants that in case of a sale he has the right to sell the materials, and that the purchasing manager (or buyer) shall have the materials free of any charge or incumbency by a third party. Ordinarily, the common law implied warranty of quality, *caveat emptor*—"let the buyer beware"—stands. However, the Uniform Sales Act, as adopted by a particular state, ordinarily provides certain exceptions to the maxim of *caveat emptor*.

Title. Title ordinarily passes when the contracting parties intend that it pass. However, in the event that the parties do not specify their intent, the common trade practice shall prevail. If there is no uniform trade practice to the contrary, the provisions of the Uniform Sales Act shall prevail. Although the provisions of this Act as adopted in any particular state may contain slight variations, the Act ordinarily provides as follows:

1. Title is ownership, not necessarily possession.
2. Ordinarily, only the owner may pass title.
3. When title passes on *specific materials* (materials set aside by the purchasing manager or buyer, or by the seller with the buyer's consent). Title passes at different times, depending upon whether the materials are (a) in a deliverable state—title ordinarily passes when the contract is made; (b) not in a deliverable state—title passes when the materials are put in a deliverable state; (c) sold on approval—title passes when the

buyer signifies his approval within an agreed-to-time or a reasonable time.

4. When title passes on *unascertained materials* (materials not set aside by the buyer or by the seller with the buyer's consent). (a) Title passes when the materials are unconditionally appropriated to the contract. (b) Title passes when delivery takes place, if prior appropriation has not occurred. Delivery to a common carrier is delivery to the buyer unless:

- The buyer names one carrier and the seller ships by another.
- The seller is required by custom or contract to deliver to the buyer himself.
- The seller is required to pay freight up to an F.O.B. point.
- The seller ships a larger or smaller quantity than that ordered.
- The seller is required by custom or contract to make arrangements with the carrier for protection of the buyer, as in a C.I.F. (cost, insurance, freight) contract.

(c) On F.O.B. shipments, title passes at the F.O.B. point. The bill of lading is evidence of title transfer. (d) On C.O.D. shipments, title passes upon delivery to the carrier, unless trade practice or the contract states to the contrary.

LEGAL ADVICE

A purchasing manager should be aware of the broad outlines and requirements of the law, and he should attempt to allow himself maximum protection by confining his activities well within the limits of the law. Another federal statute of special concern to a purchasing manager is the Robinson-Patman Act, which amends Section 2 of the Clayton Act of 1914 to read as follows:

> That it shall be unlawful for any person engaged in commerce . . . either directly or indirectly to discriminate in

price between different purchasers of commodities of the like grade and quality where . . . the effect of such discrimination may be to substantially lessen competition or tend to create a monopoly in any line of commerce, or to injure, destroy, or prevent competition with any person who either grants or knowingly receives the benefit of such discrimination or with customers of either of them. . . .

Furthermore, the Act makes it illegal to "knowingly induce or receive" a discriminatory price. Price differentials are allowable for the following reasons:

1. Differences in cost of manufacture, sale, or delivery resulting from differing methods of manufacture or quantities in which the commodity is sold.
2. Differences in quality.
3. Changed economic or seasonal conditions.
4. "Unloading" of perishable or obsolete items.
5. Distress or "going out of business" sales.
6. Offering a price to meet the equally low price of a competitor.

It is important to note that a party injured by price discrimination may sue the injuring party for "triple damages."

The significance of the Robinson-Patman Act to purchasing managers is that while most of the restrictions appear to affect suppliers, they can also be employed against a buyer if he uses his purchasing power to knowingly cause price discrimination or restrain competition.

MEASUREMENT OF PURCHASING

The development of an effective means of measuring purchasing performance is a difficult task. The very nature of the purchasing function makes it so. Ways and means of measurement vary widely from company to company, but they are usually limited in scope. It is often rather like checking the oil in a car and declaring, "The motor is in great shape." It is a fact that we can measure many things in a purchasing department, but not everything. Purchasing managers are confused, and no wonder. They hear one prominent purchasing executive advocate measurement by objectives, and another, equally prominent, advocate measurement by results. Then there are others who say that purchasing should concern itself mainly with modern techniques, and let the results speak for themselves—sort of measurement by default.

A standard of measurement quoted most often is to get the right goods at the right time and at the right price. Many people involved in the purchasing function use this measurement as the sole criterion of whether they are doing a good job. The time has long since passed for this to be considered the only effective measurement. Through the years many companies were satisfied with this simple standard, as poor as it was, because it was an improvement over the loose methods of former years. Most managers will agree that the slow development and refinement of the purchasing function was due largely to its second-class status in the company and the lack of interest by top management. In many instances this was evidenced by the personnel employed in the purchasing function—personnel who generally had only a clerical background that limited their ability and their desire to do much more than maintain records of orders placed and expedite rush orders. It seems almost inconceivable that one of the key operations of a company—purchasing—has been so casually organized and staffed. Fortunately, in most companies the value of a good purchasing operation has been recognized, and positive steps have been taken to correct the deficiencies.

The answers to the following questions can be useful in measuring the efficiency of some aspects of the purchasing function. The greater the objectivity and accuracy exercised in obtaining answers to these questions, the greater the likelihood that the conclusions reached will be sound.

1. Do you have an up-to-date organization chart of your purchasing operation—one that clearly defines the duties and responsibilities of each employee?

2. Do you have standards to control rush orders, or is money wasted by the indiscriminate use of such orders?

3. Are all purchases made against written requisitions, or do you accept verbal requests?

4. Are requisitions signed by someone in authority or by almost anyone?

5. Do you have a simplified method of placing small orders, or is the cost of processing the purchase order greater than the cost of the materials purchased?

6. Are all contacts with suppliers handled initially by purchasing, or is the time of other managers wasted needlessly?

7. Do you have a purchasing budget or any other plan that can be used as a guide to measure effectiveness?

8. Do you have a follow-up system, or do you only learn that materials were not delivered if there is a delay in production?

9. Are receiving and inspection set up for the most efficient flow of work?

10. Do you know the most profitable rate of turnover for each item in inventory, or are you losing money due to over- or understocking?

11. Do your purchasing records reflect prices and complete supplier information, or do you have to guess when to reorder?

12. Have you analyzed the underlying causes of what you feel is your major headache?

At this point we should profit by reviewing several examples that illustrate the difficulty in measuring purchasing. Let's assume that a purchasing manager attempts to control the quality of a widget purchased regularly. What standard of measurement can he use? Perhaps the most feasible is the percentage of widgets rejected per month by inspection. Thus if the supplier's rejection rate remains at or below the standard, this indicates that the purchasing manager has selected a widget and a supplier that satisfy the user's needs. So far, so good. However, is this the extent of the purchasing manager's responsibility? Is it possible for him to locate a more satisfactory widget, from the aspect of quality as related to function, if he studies the user's needs more carefully and investigates the widgets of other suppliers? The most important feature of a good purchasing manager is his ability to go beyond the simple purchase of a satisfactory widget.

The price factor is clearly related to the quality factor in the preceding example. Suppose the purchasing manager also wants to control the price paid for the widget. He can probably establish a standard price by studying the market, but how meaningful will this standard be? Does it reflect the fact that a widget of lower quality and price may be acceptable? Does it reflect the potential price reduction that the purchasing manager may obtain by using a detailed cost analysis in negotiating with the supplier? Does it reflect the pricing improvement that may be gained from more skillful grouping of commodities?

As you can see, it is difficult to establish absolute quantitative standards of measurement in the majority of situations; the accuracy and validity of such standards are open to question in many instances. The intangible nature of purchasing's primary responsibilities prohibits the direct measurement of purchasing accomplishment.

Most standards of measurement, therefore, focus on secondary factors that are only *indications* of accomplishment. Secondary factors that can be measured, such as quality, rejection rate, and price paid, are useful in determining performance trends, but they may not be especially useful in appraising the absolute level of accomplishment. In each specific case the validity factor must be assessed.

Because of the difficulty of developing precise controls of purchasing, many companies have adopted a fairly broad approach that possesses three distinctive features. The first involves a qualitative assessment of several broad management responsibilities, such as the capabilities of personnel, the soundness of organizational structure, and plans and policies in purchasing. The theory underlying such an evaluation is that these factors control the potential level of purchasing department performance; as such, they are useful indirect indicators of performance.

The second feature embraces attempts to establish performance standards for the measurable secondary factors related to primary purchasing objectives. The fact is that many companies recognize that one factor alone may not provide a true indication of creative purchasing performance, and, accordingly, they develop a cross check by measuring several factors that relate to the same objective. As an example, purchasing performance relative to the price objective can be checked from two standpoints: (1) Actual prices paid can be compared with target prices, and (2) targets for cost savings resulting from negotiation and value analysis can be established and actual savings compared with them. Thus two measurements provide a cross check on the same objective—price.

The third feature of the broad approach deals with purchasing efficiency. Skill in purchasing and efficiency in purchasing are two distinctly different factors. Efficiency control involves evaluation of workloads, utilization of personnel, operating costs, and processing times as related to specific volumes of purchasing operations. A purchasing manager clearly wants to achieve a high degree of operating efficiency, but not at the expense of purchasing skill. Thorough competence is a concern with cost, price, and human relationships; competence offers far more opportunity for savings than mere efficiency.

In essence, the broad approach is nothing but a management analysis of the purchasing function. In evaluating or measuring purchasing performance, top management, an outside consultant, or a good purchasing manager will ask the following questions:

1. Do all purchasing personnel understand the department's objectives?

2. Do you have two-way communication with management?

3. Is all purchasing activity centralized in the purchasing department? Have clear lines of authority and responsibility been established? Is there adequate planning to meet future needs?

4. Are adequate selection criteria used in hiring personnel? What planning and preparation are done for advancement and replacement of personnel? Is compensation adequate?

5. Does purchasing participate in the formulation of policies on forward buying, reciprocity, and inventory levels? To what extent does purchasing participate in make-or-buy decisions?

6. Is a policy manual in use? Is a well-defined purchasing policy of responsibility and authority well known and accepted throughout the company?

7. Are adequate records (with an emphasis on product and supplier records) maintained to facilitate effective purchasing?

You, as a purchasing manager, should not forfeit the many advantages of evaluation and control simply because of the admitted inaccuracies of measurement and results that fall short of perfection. There are no easy answers in measuring purchasing performance. But if the purchasing manager tailors his system to basic principles, the results he obtains will be that much more valid.

RESISTANCE TO CHANGE

Reliable sources claim that more man-hours and money are spent on managing company affairs than on any other activity. For the most part, this managerial leadership is undertaken without special training in the skills required to cope with change. As a result, the behavior of those people attempting to achieve change often creates an impenetrable barrier between the people they are trying to guide and themselves. Such a condition exists even though numerous management development programs are in operation today and increasing numbers of people in managerial positions have college degrees or have studied at some other educational institution.

A major reason for the dearth of more effective leadership is a lack of ability on the part of modern managers to cope with the rapid process of change that is taking place in today's business or industrial organization. We live in a world of rapid change. In less than two decades, modern technology has leaped from conventional to nuclear power, from the piston to the jet age, and has converted "earth men" into "space men." Change brings with it challenges for those who manage people.

Clarence B. Randall, former board chairman of Inland Steel Company, has laid the blame for much of the failure to cope with change squarely on management's own doorstep:

> The timorous and hard pressed executive, who deep down inside resents and resists change—seeks refuge in meaningless statistics. Not sure of his own thinking and hesitant to plunge boldly ahead on a plan that would put his personal status in hazard, he takes protective covering in conformity with whatever general level of conduct seems to be emerging.*

Coping with change mainly involves the proper understanding and utilization of the human resources in an organization. An organization can be described as a way in which people arrange themselves in terms of their relationships with others in order to get something important accomplished, either for themselves or for society. An industrial organization is such an arrangement. Its goal is the manufacture and distribution of a consumable product.

Success in achieving improved productivity, greater effi-

* Clarence B. Randall, "The Myth of the Magic Numbers," *Dun's Review of Modern Industry* (March 1961), p. 34.

ciency, or better service depends on management's ability to utilize human resources in order to cope with the changing demands of the organization. What is this basic human resource upon which so much depends? It is the individual; a single, complex organism working in a variety of ways to supply his own needs. He can do this alone, or in informal or formal face-to-face groups made up of other individuals working in a variety of ways to supply their needs. Frustration is experienced by those who think success in mobilizing human resources is simply a matter of education and, perhaps, of using persuasive stimuli reinforced by annual picnics, newsletters, and adequate coffee breaks.

A newly identified but actually old-fashioned key to obtaining commitment for a new idea, method, or procedure is the involvement of the individuals in face-to-face situations for the purpose of self-determination. This general principle is best explained within specific guidelines about the process of change. We know a great deal about change. Many useful beginnings have been made and various approaches to problems of social change have been suggested. Research and experience by social scientists have provided some guidelines as to why people resist change. However, in this discussion the contention is that *people do not resist change itself; rather, they balk at the methods used to effect change.*

No longer can we shrug our shoulders and say, "You can't change people." Research shows that we *can* change people. In fact, people like change. They resist because of the methods that managers use to put changes into effect. When people fear change it is because it upsets their way of doing things and threatens their security. However, this feeling is balanced by a desire for new experiences and for the benefits that come as a result of change.

Let us examine in more detail some of the reasons for this resistance. People resent change when—

- *The purpose is not made clear.* Mystery and ambiguity cause suspense and anxiety. Fear of change can be as disrupting as change itself, because it produces identical worries and unrest.

- *They are not involved in the planning.* It's only human nature to support what we create. We're all ready to follow our own suggestions.
- *An appeal is based on personal reasons.* The manager who says to his men, "Won't you come through for good old David?" is met with suspicion. The attitude immediately is, "What's David getting out of this?" Loyalty is a desirable trait in subordinates, but few people will change just because of it. They will respond to a personal plea only if, at the same time, they see that it solves a problem—gets something done—reaches a goal.
- *The habit patterns of the work group are ignored.* The warehouse equipment drivers and stock men who can talk to each other as they work side by side, the group of office girls who eat lunch together, the utility crew that has appropriated a favorite truck—all are stubbornly against anything that will alter their working relationship.
- *There is poor communication regarding a change.* Even though a change will affect only one or two in a work group, all of them need to know about the change in order to feel secure and to maintain group cooperation.
- *There is fear of failure.* Today people are predominantly concerned with whether they have the ability to master new skills. Fear of failure is especially strong when people are threatened with punishment such as demotion, loss of status, lower pay, or the displeasure of the boss.
- *Excessive work pressure is involved.* Often such pressure results when we don't plan for changes far enough in advance, or are uneasy about the change ourselves.
- *The cost is too high, or the reward for making the change is seen as inadequate.* For example, people without children may be reluctant to vote for a school bond issue, even though they approve of better schools, because it may raise their taxes.

- *The present situation seems satisfactory.* It's only human nature to take the attitude, "Don't stick your neck out," or "We never had it so good," or "Why upset the apple cart?"

In light of these factors, what can a manager do to initiate and cope with change? Let's examine a few conditions which have been found to lessen resistance to change. First, a number of studies have indicated that there is less resistance when people are allowed to convince themselves that change is needed. This, of course, requires adequate communication so that no one is surprised or caught off guard and feels that something has been put over on him. If people are involved in the diagnostic and creative planning stages of the proposed change, they will be more apt to understand and support the change because they helped create it. Thus if they help make the diagnosis, they more readily accept the prognosis—which is to say that employees can seldom be treated as a doctor treats a patient, by mysterious prescription.

Second, change comes more easily when there is some provision for people to blow off steam generated by their resistance. Many managers have tried to move ahead fast so that the opposition doesn't get a chance to organize. Third, motivation affects a person's willingness to be an effective human resource—to give or not to give of himself to his organization. Resistance may be reduced if the following factors are seriously considered:

Meaningful reward. This varies with individuals. They may be concerned with self-expression, recognition, the need to feel useful and important, the desire for new knowledge, the need to meet new people, or a genuine desire to meet the needs of the company.

Relationship. However small it may be, the individual must be able to relate his contribution to a total effort.

Importance. Has the contribution had any real meaning to the organization, or was it a wasted effort? The individual may not particularly care whether the answer to this question is happily "yes" or miserably "no," but he does want to feel that he himself is important enough to be informed as to the final outcome, and he doesn't want to repeat wasted effort. He works best in a warm but work-oriented atmosphere where his efforts are obviously needed and appreciated.

Initial success. A little success goes a long way toward maintaining interest in new ways of doing things. The jobs people are given to do must be within their skills and experience, because frustration at the outset is sure death to the efforts to stabilize or initiate change.

Opportunity to grow. Interest stops when stagnation is produced by doing the same thing repeatedly; and continued involvement demands new challenges to learn and grow.

Appropriate involvement in decision making. People should be allowed to take part in this process. One of the most difficult jobs a manager has is to refrain from making most of the decisions by himself.

Keep people informed. When an individual contributes even a small response, he automatically develops an interest in what happens to it. He will feel more intimately involved if he shares in the knowledge of what the organization's problems as well as its achievements are.

Fourth, be certain that people know the goals of or reasons for the change. You may have heard the story of an executive who successfully initiated a change in his staff. He carefully planned how to tell them all the whys and wherefores and had answers to all the ifs, ands, and buts. Later, as he advanced in his job, he failed miserably when he had to sell a group of his managers on a change. Why? He felt that because of their superior intelligence, they would not need an explanation. But the fact that people are intelligent does not necessarily mean they will better understand and accept change. Often the opposite is true. They may use their intelligence to find even more reasons why a change should not be made.

Goals become confused when people are confronted with too many trivial and unnecessary changes. People can tolerate only so much change, and if they are bombarded with small innovations and changes, they will be less apt to accept major changes.

Fifth, build a work climate of trust. Mistrust arises when people have inadequate or incomplete information, when they are kept in the dark, or when rumors disseminate false alarms. One major reason is that they feel helpless—they can't influence the situation. To create a better climate, tell the truth. It has been proved time and again that people would rather have bad news than no news. Given the facts, they feel they can do something about the problem.

And finally, don't be afraid to err. Too many managers are so afraid of making mistakes that they rigidify their organization with checks and counterchecks, discourage innovation, and, in the end, so structure themselves that they often miss the kind of offbeat opportunity that can send a firm skyrocketing.

THE CYCLE OF PURCHASING MANAGEMENT

To understand the unique problems of purchasing management, we should consider some of the attempts that have been made to define and describe a good purchasing manager. If you are a truly effective purchasing manager, you establish purchasing goals and objectives, and follow through on them; negotiate contracts for groups of materials rather than for individual items (unless, of course, the individual item is of a large volume); communicate clearly—with your own purchasing department personnel, with other departments, and with top management; and maintain a close relationship with suppliers, visiting suppliers' plants when feasible. A good manager is a man who inspires people of ordinary ability to perform in an extraordinary manner. You elicit more work and a better performance willingly from those under you. You take more risks, and you encourage and enjoy the process of change rather than routine.

As a good manager you make every effort to keep the ablest

minds in your department continually growing in their capacity as decision makers. By putting more responsibilities on your assistants' shoulders, you create a need for and stimulate your personal growth. A good manager is one who gets things done both *through* others and *with* others.

There are, of course, other characteristics of a good manager: *flexibility* in planning alternatives and visualizing possible contingencies; *simplicity,* knowing how to cut problems down to size; and the art of discipline. When it becomes necessary to put a man on the carpet, you have your facts straight and your prescription for improvement clearly outlined. Discipline should not be designed to punish but rather to persuade a man to do better. The good manager knows that discipline should be administered in private, never in the presence of fellow-workers.

THE IMPORTANCE OF LISTENING

In purchasing, more than in any other department, much of your time is taken up in listening to salesmen. But efficient listening is very difficult. No matter how closely you listen, a person is able to understand clearly the precise meaning of only 600–900 words in a ten-minute conversation. Our thinking speed far exceeds our listening rate, and since we're usually ahead of the speaker, our thoughts often wander while we wait for him to catch up. Another obstacle we encounter is that of bias. Objective listening is complicated by the fact that we interpret what we hear in terms of our prejudices, our mood, and our attitude toward the person speaking.

A few suggestions for overcoming roadblocks to listening may be helpful. *Be receptive.* Listen to new ideas even though they may clash with your present way of thinking. *Concentrate.* Follow the thread of ideas from the initial sentence to the conclusion. *Become involved.* As the speaker goes on, maintain a running mental summary of his points. *Ask questions.* Make sure that you clarify all the speaker's points. *Prepare.* If you know that the conversation is going to be of a technical nature, make every attempt to secure background information in advance.

MOTIVATION

The actions that our companies, and we as purchasing managers, take to cause our people to do the best work of which they are capable are the foundation of motivation. The problem of achieving the best kind of working relationships with personnel should be foremost in the mind of every purchasing manager. The following "Ten Commandments of Motivation" may be helpful to you in accomplishing this goal.

1. Know each employee as an individual and as a person, and show your personal interest.
2. Establish fair standards, and let him know exactly what you expect of him.
3. Let him know constantly where he stands and how he's doing.
4. Praise him publicly, rebuke him privately. Respect and enhance his dignity.
5. Insist on high work standards; recognize good work and poor performance promptly.
6. Tell him, in advance, of changes that affect him.
7. Deal him in on what's going on; not only talk but listen.
8. Give him equality of opportunity and assignments that recognize and challenge his abilities.
9. Play no favorites; keep your promises.
10. Earn his respect through your competence, firmness, and fairness.

MEETINGS

You have probably heard the saying, "a committee should consist of three people, two of whom should be absent." It sometimes seems that the same principle should be applied to meetings. We often seem to have a meeting about a meeting! Complaints about the problem of business meetings are getting like complaints about the weather; everybody talks about it, but no one seems to be able to do anything about it.

Many of the meetings held within our companies are too long, lack planning and organization, and are not used as problem-solving tools. Instead, meetings or conferences often serve as a way to avoid taking responsibility, making decisions, and accepting possible blame, or as an excuse for casual socializing. An effective and efficient purchasing manager must be aware of what makes a meeting tick. The following points may be helpful:

- Keep the tone of the meeting objective and unbiased to bring out ideas. A meeting is best conducted in an atmosphere free of emotional conflict.
- Establish objectives. Meeting leaders and participants should have a clear, concise, and realistic definition of the purpose and objective to be achieved.
- Consider other means to the end. Could letters, telephone calls, or other methods be just as effective?
- Keep an idea file. Whenever an idea pertinent to the meeting occurs, jot it down for the future planning stage.
- Select the chairman or leader carefully. He should have adequate knowledge of the subject, efficiency in presentation, skill in directing a group, and the ability to prepare and summarize the discussion.
- Use an agenda. Prepare an agenda to cover such points as the "when, where, who, what, why, and how long."
- Select the participants. A good rule of thumb is to include only those essential for achieving objectives.
- Give out premeeting assignments. Ask the participants to prime themselves in advance by digging into the problem. Bring data required.

One very important point—don't have a meeting for the sake of a meeting. A meeting that is inadequately planned usually results in no decisions, and thus it is a complete waste of valuable time.

Discipline

Good discipline is a reasonable goal and a definite responsibility of every purchasing manager. It is absolutely necessary for the success of an organization as a profit-making business. However, discipline does not mean cracking the whip so personnel leap through hoops upon command, or cursing them out so they know their place. What, then, is a measure of good discipline? If your personnel willingly, promptly, and cheerfully live up to company rules, you have good discipline. If you can leave your operation and know that the work will go on as though you were still there, you have good discipline.

Discipline cannot be bought. Discipline cannot be imposed by force. Discipline cannot be "required." Discipline can only be obtained by earning it. In the final analysis, discipline is actually a matter of cooperation with and respect for you, the company, and the company's rules.

The following are some basic methods for insuring good discipline: Make certain that *you* know the company's rules, that *you* understand them, and that *you* know why they are necessary, and then be certain that every employee knows these same things as well as you do. Every employee must be properly instructed in the proper work methods and practices, and orders and instructions that you give should always be clear and easily understood. Make certain that each employee is capable of handling the assignment given him. Each employee must be treated equally, with no favoritism or prejudice.

You must be alert to potential violations of discipline, and attempt to prevent them before they occur. Be quite sure that your evaluation of a violation is accurate, fair, and thorough, and then correct the violation promptly and in a businesslike and mutually respectful manner. Make certain that profit is obtained from the correction, that improvement is gained by all concerned, and that repetition is unlikely. Follow up by being alert to improved discipline, and be ready to give appropriate personal compliments. Make certain that you restrain your temper and act the part of a mature, sensible, and responsible purchasing manager. As a manager of people, you won't have to get tough if you've done your homework. Remember, discipline is not punishment—it is preventive action. Good purchasing management requires good rules, and good rules require good humane application and administration.

CREATIVITY

Creative purchasing managers rise to the top of the executive pyramid. You must stimulate a continual flow of new ideas and ask your subordinates to do so as well. People who have been successful idea-getters say that the best approach is to find the time of day when you're most creative—the time when you're full of drive. For some it's in the morning; for others it's in the evening. Build up your sources for ideas by reading trade magazines, visiting suppliers' plants, and attending conventions and conferences. Don't be afraid to work alone. Creative thinking isn't necessarily a group process. However, you should have the courage to put your ideas to the test of criticism, which can be an excellent stimulant for creativity.

Beware of self-satisfaction. Matt Russ, formerly regional vice-president and now executive vice-president of The Macke Company, credits his region's success to the "inquiring mind" approach to problems. "This point of view is never satisfied with things as they are," he says. "We assumed that anything and everything—product, process, methods, procedures, or human relations—could be improved."

You must organize your approach. When replacing a machine or process ask yourself these questions: Will it do more? Will it be more reliable, last longer, be easier to repair and maintain, be safer, and be more efficient? Will it cost less? Will it be easier to sell?

Your willpower controls your imagination and is affected by your emotions. Build faith in yourself by scoring successes on small problems before tackling big ones. Be enthusiastic and be confident. It is important to relax your mind after a hard day's work—let it wander. Think of ideas while driving to and from work, while showering, or while listening to restful music. If your mind becomes clogged, set your problem aside for a day or so, then hit it again.

Don't worry about the opinion of others. A couple of bicycle mechanics by the name of Wright would never have gotten their airplane off the ground if they had listened to the physicists of their day. On the other hand, the man who recognizes a mistake finds out why he made it and corrects it while learning how to do things differently. Learn to spot mistakes. Listen to complaints. Jot down your own complaints about the way things are done in your department. Seek better methods.

Talk it over with others. Sometimes the simplest way to get ideas is by going to other people for help. They will often give you a fresh slant on your problem. All ideas are elusive. They will drift out of your mind as readily as they drifted in. Carry a pad and pencil or, better yet, a tape recorder with you.

Above all, don't be an uncreative purchasing manager. A creative manager will let his people expand their jobs; the uncreative manager will keep his subordinates in their niches with rigid job descriptions.

WHY SOME PURCHASING MANAGERS FAIL

You no doubt have known a man who had been an excellent buyer but failed miserably as a purchasing manager. Why? One of the most common reasons for failure is the inability to delegate responsibility. The man who tries to do all the work himself spends so much time on details that he has too little time left for more important things such as forecasting market conditions, developing sound supplier relationships,

and negotiating deals on volume items. Furthermore, he hasn't oriented himself to total corporate objectives. His expertise as a buyer in managing requisitions and purchase orders required technical skill, and he fails to recognize that the responsibilities of purchasing management involve leading, planning, and controlling the efforts of others.

ARE YOU LIKED AS A PURCHASING MANAGER?

One of the most respected men in purchasing today, Victor H. Pooler, Jr., says, "Purchasing is, indeed, a friction-producing job."* If you are thought of as a great fellow you had better watch out! It could be a sign of trouble ahead.

Unless you're modest to the extreme, you probably have a fairly good opinion of yourself as a purchasing manager. All the right adjectives come to mind. Informed. Decisive. Agreeable to work with, and, above all, well thought of by almost all your subordinates, associates, and superiors. But what if you're dead wrong? What if it's true that your subordinates like you, but it's because they think of you as a soft touch? Or, maybe the reason you find your associates so agreeable is that they consider you too hard-headed and set in your ways to argue with. And take a good look at the "nice" way your superiors treat you. It could be that, even though they've written you off for future promotions, they think you're perfect in your present position—for good.

If any of these things are true about you, the odds are high that you will be the last to find out. That's because most people, particularly in the business world, have perfected innumerable ways of hiding their feelings. If you want to ferret out the truth about yourself as a purchasing manager, you'll have to do it yourself. Take a very close look at the way people respond to you. The way subordinates respond to your orders.

* Victor H. Pooler, Jr., *The Purchasing Man and His Job* (A.M.A., 1964), p. 29.

Is their usual reaction something less than snappy and enthusiastic and more like an unspoken "keep your shirt on, I'll get to it when I'm good and ready"? The way your associates respond to you when you're at the conference table. Do your plans and ideas ever inspire close attention and spark lively discussion, or do they usually provoke glassy stares or suggestions to "break for lunch"? And, finally, the way your superiors *really* regard you. This doesn't mean how they welcome you to their offices or smile in the corridors, but whether they consistently assign you important tasks that need fast, sure action, and whether they have solid confidence in your decisions and recommendations.

In short, all these people who "like" you so much may be telling you, in small but nevertheless vivid ways, that you haven't got what it takes. Is there anything that you can do about it? Is it possible to make a careful study of your business personality and take positive steps to eliminate your shortcomings and magnify your assets? Can you, in effect, make yourself into a better purchasing manager with new powers in motivating and influencing people? The answer is an emphatic *yes*—provided that you're willing to make the effort. How? By attending as many seminars, workshops, and courses in purchasing management as possible. Such educational opportunities are offered continually by the American Management Association, the National Association of Purchasing Management, local associations affiliated with NAPM, and many colleges and universities. Purchasing education is a never-ending activity. Participation, at least once each year, in a purchasing course can be a most valuable and rewarding experience.

CONCLUSION

We have come full circle in our discussion of the many duties, responsibilities, and problems of a purchasing manager. Rather than summarize what has already been stated at length in the preceding sections, perhaps it would be more helpful to conclude this book with a few thoughts that have not been covered and with a look into the future.

True progress will be paced by the availability of willing and able people working together in the pursuit of common, preselected goals. The capable person is our most precious corporate asset. One of the biggest complaints I have concerning purchasing people, from buyers through purchasing vice-presidents, is the fact that, while many do a superb job, they fail miserably in not "tooting their own horn." If you're a winner, let management know it. The news about your accomplishments, and the recognition it brings, will benefit you, your department, and your company. However, I do mean honest news—reports on negotiated savings that resulted in a direct contribution to the bottom line of the profit and loss statement, for example.

Also, fight for your programs just as the accounting and engineering fellows fight for theirs. You cannot sit quietly on the sidelines and expect top management to know what you're thinking. I'm sure many of you know executives who by simply laying it on the line with management get all the assistants and other clerical help they need. Organize and summarize the things done by your department, pick out the vital statistics, and avoid the trivia. To be effective, a purchasing manager must understand total company problems. You should examine every area that shows promise of improvement. Even though you reach a point where there appear to be more problems than there are solutions, remain steadfast in your search for a better way. Don't let yourself be pushed into a short-term solution, because often a long-term solution may prove to be more profitable.

Furthermore, don't let steadily rising prices fool you; you have more negotiating leverage than you think. There are some fast and simple ways to expand and make better use of that leverage along the way. There is really no magic to the method —just be alert to what your suppliers are pushing and saying; then do a little reading between the lines. Invariably, your suppliers will hand you the additional leverage you need to swing a deal. You see, suppliers are being prodded by the same profit pinch and uncertain business prospects that you are. Therefore, where your two areas of interest meet, you have the makings of a mutually beneficial transaction. Remember, a major area to investigate is the consolidation of like items to secure volume. You need volume to secure better prices and better terms. Another area to look into would be year-long contracts based on annual volume. You will find that you have more leverage now than you've ever had.

We are entering an age which will demand creative leadership in an environment of continuing change. The accent will be on team problem-solving and responsive, flexible organization. To prosper, purchasing managers must be a part of the professional management team. We stand free to create and lead; or we stand chained by our failure to act.

The unique purchasing functions will be carried out by career specialists who are professionally trained to lead and direct the performance of the many tasks which fall within the scope of purchasing. It is likely that the prime purchasing functions will be clustered within three different organizational levels, and the emphasis will shift at each level.

At the purchasing staff level, the development and maintenance of required human assets will receive prime consideration.

At the corporate level, the various elements of company operation must be considered as interrelated parts of the total corporate plan; and their worth must be measured in relation to the contribution each makes to the achievement of the stated long-range objectives of the company. Personnel assigned within this second level of purchasing activity will lead, coordinate, and control the selection and development of key suppliers who, although small in total number, will represent the greatest share of external contractual purchasing commitments of the company. The purchasing department's accountability for contracting with key suppliers will probably reside at the apex of profit-center departments. Moreover, it is likely that purchasing personnel at this level will focus their attention upon obtaining clear definitions of the materials and services required from suppliers, and upon the prime purchasing job of negotiating and awarding key contracts.

Personnel assigned to the third organizational level will be closely aligned to the general area of purchase contract administration and inventory flow. Their prime interest will be in supplying materials from preselected suppliers according to established purchase contract terms. The accent will be upon inventory control and lead-time control. This will be a computer-supported operation, and it will be in sharp contrast to the paper-shuffling, trivia-submerged purchasing operation of the past.

THE SUCCESSFUL PURCHASING MANAGER

Perhaps the following checklist will help you answer that all-important question: "Am I doing my job well?" You are an effective, efficient purchasing manager who is performing his job well when you can honestly say that you—

1. Constantly evaluate the impact of individual purchasing actions upon the total momentum of the company.
2. Measure activities and results in terms of their impact upon the achievement of corporate or company goals.
3. Think first of people and the way they work together toward common objectives, because you know that the machines are merely support tools but the people are the creative assets of the company.
4. Have a more than casual understanding of the marketing activities of your suppliers and potential suppliers.
5. Have an awareness of product developments and of the competitive posture of your company.

174

6. Are alert to the rapidly advancing state of purchasing knowledge. Consequently, you will probably spend at least 10 percent of your time pursuing further education in the purchasing field.

Finally, if as purchasing manager you become a specialist in anything, it will be in the art of negotiation, leadership, and general administration. You must become familiar with new tools, such as computers, to help you do a better job.

THE CONTINUING CHALLENGE

Do you ever feel that there ought to be a point where as a purchasing manager you really have it made? A point at which your contributions have been so outstanding that you ought to be able to relax and enjoy a free ride the rest of the way? Well, maybe there should be, but there isn't! The minute a purchasing manager begins to relax, he begins to lose his value. Someone else, with more drive and ambition, could possibly step in and do a better job in your place.

As Matt Russ, Executive Vice-President of the Macke Company, says, "What a man accomplished yesterday is water over the dam. More important now is what you can do for the company today and tomorrow. When the things you did yesterday and last year are more important than your ambitions for tomorrow and next year, it's time to let someone else take over." This may sound like a hard, unfeeling way to look at things, but isn't it the truth? You can't win today's game on last week's press clippings. No success is final—no success can last forever. The purchasing manager who enjoys success has to plan to keep on succeeding. As each goal is achieved, he must look for a new one; that's what makes life interesting. But, as today's teenagers would put it, he must also "hang loose," not be uptight.

When you feel as though you've got it made, watch out! It's the first step toward settling back into a pleasant, convenient rut. The man who "has it made" is only a step away from becoming a "has-been." Certainly, one of the tragedies of business today is the fact that quite a number of employees have mentally retired. They are resting on their laurels; they aren't looking for new challenges; they are not interested in ways of doing things more cheaply or better. They have long forgotten why their company is in business in the first place. So keep alive—keep challenging yourself and your personnel and you will be rewarded.

In closing I quote from a plaque given to me by a very close personal friend, William E. Poindexter: "The science of business is the science of service; he profits most who serves the best. To this end, it is better to do more than you promise, than to promise more than you do."

Appendixes

Employee Evaluation Report – Exempt

CATEGORY: V – WAGE AND SALARY
SUBJECT: EMPLOYEE PERFORMANCE AND POTENTIAL
APPRAISAL – EXEMPT

.01 It is the policy of The Macke Company to evaluate the performance and potential of all exempt personnel on a periodic basis. The purpose of this measure is to:

A. Determine and to constructively inform the person being appraised how effective he has been in carrying out assigned company objectives.

B. Determine his potential for work in broader or on higher levels of responsibility.

C. Identify the type and amount of assistance he requires to make him more effective on his present job, or to prepare him for promotion.

D. Develop and implement a joint plan of action to fulfill his needs through training or guided experience. This will involve the employee, his supervisor and the training department.

E. Motivate the employee to self-development and to higher levels of performance, quality of work and productivity.

.02 A performance and potential appraisal may be accomplished at any time. However, appraisals will be completed at the following times:

- 6 months from date of hire, transfer, promotion or demotion.
- 12 months from date of hire, transfer, promotion or demotion.
- Annually thereafter.
- At time of promotion.
- At time of demotion.

.03 The appraisal form will be originated by the Industrial Relations Department and sent to the employee's supervisor for completion at 6 months, 12 months and annually thereafter. All other appraisals will be initiated by the department concerned. The forms will be distributed at least fifteen (15) days prior to the due date of the appraisal.

Accompanying the appraisal form will be a copy of the employee's job description, which is to be reviewed by the supervisor for completeness and accuracy.

.04 The following steps should be taken in completing the appraisal.

A. Prior to filling out the form, review the individual's job description and performance standards/objectives. Make sure that you have the total job in mind and that you examine his performance over the entire period of the appraisal rather than just the last few weeks.

B. Fill out the form. Be objective and specific in your remarks. Focus on his success or failure in achieving results and not on his personal characteristics. The exception to this would be the case where characteristics interfere with the achievement of results. Take as much time as is necessary to do the job right.

C. Upon completion of the written appraisal, review it with your immediate superior so that any problems or questions are reconciled prior to the appraisal interview. This is also a good time to discuss any pending action such as a promotion, transfer or discharge. The more you know the better able you will be to conduct an effective interview.

D. Give the employee an opportunity to review the form prior to the appraisal interview. He will sign the form indicating that he has reviewed it.

E. Conduct the appraisal interview. This is the most important part of the appraisal process and, therefore, it should be given particular attention. The climate of the interview should be positive and helpful. With clearly stated job objectives, it should not be difficult to conduct the interview on a positive note. The employee should know where he stands in relation to his objectives and can be asked how he is doing rather being told. The following are recommended steps in the interview:

(1) Discuss achievements and strengths. Start the interview on as positive a basis as possible.

(2) Discuss weaknesses or needs.

(3) Get agreement on a development plan, including specific events, dates and what is actually to be accomplished.

(4) Assure the employee of his ability to achieve (if this is the case).

.05 After the interview is completed, forward the appraisal form to the Industrial Relations Department. When a Personnel Action Notice is required, attach it to the appraisal and send it to the Industrial Relations Department for final review.

THE MACKE COMPANY
EXEMPT EMPLOYEE PERFORMANCE AND POTENTIAL APPRAISA

Region: _____

Name: _____ Company: _____

Branch: _____

Position: _____ Reports to: _____

Length of Service in Position Rated:____Total Years of Service:____

Present Weekly Salary:___Effective Date:___Date of This Rating:___

REASON FOR REVIEW:

_____ 6 months from date of (hire) (transfer) (promotion) (demotion)
_____ 12 months from date of (hire) (transfer) (promotion) (demotion)
_____ Annual review
_____ Promotion
_____ Demotion

PART I – REVIEW OF JOB OBJECTIVES

What are his job objectives? (What have you and he agreed would be
accomplished on the job as of this appraisal)? _____

_____

_____

_____

_____

_____

_____

_____

PART II – APPRAISAL OF CURRENT PERFORMANCE

What were his major job accomplishments during the period being
evaluated? (How has he improved or failed to improve since last
appraisal? How well has he met his job objectives?) _____

_____

_____

_____

_____

_____

_____

_____

PART III – SUPERVISORY ABILITY

If employee is a supervisor (one or more subordinates), how effective has he been in controlling his subordinate(s) performance on the following items?

E – Excellent   AA – Above Average   S – Satisfactory
          F – Fair   U – Unsatisfactory

	E	AA	S	F	U	
Absenteeism						
Tardiness						
Safety – Accident frequency						
Accident severity						
Spoilage (if applicable)						
Shortages (if applicable)						
Theft (if applicable)						
Management upgrade (preparation of his subordinates for higher level responsibilities)						
Grievances						
Budget control (if applicable)						
Suggestion system						

PART IV – PERFORMANCE APPRAISAL CATEGORIES

Read each of the performance appraisal categories which describe levels of performance. Determine which category most accurately describes the performance level of the employee and circle the appropriate number.

1. OUTSTANDING – Performance which is consistently and unquestionably far above the level normally expected of a "fully satisfactory" performer – and most, if not all, other employees. Other employees will generally recognize this competence and look to this employee for guidance. By definition alone, the total number of qualifiers for this performance rating will be limited to a relatively select few. It is from this group that candidates for immediate promotion to available openings in higher rated positions are normally selected; thereby further reducing the number who would ever reach the maximum rate.

2. ABOVE AVERAGE – Overall performance is, on a sustained basis, significantly above the level normally achieved by employees whose performance is fully satisfactory. This level of performance predicts rapid development and indicates consideration for advancement to a position of greater responsibility.

3. FULLY SATISFACTORY — This is the employee whose performance of the job requirements is "fully satisfactory," but who doesn't "stand out in a crowd," either as a top producer or a problem. This level of performance would not merit consideration for promotion but with additional training and coaching may result in performing the present job better.

4. SATISFACTORY AVERAGE — This is the employee whose performance just merits the minimum performance requirements of the job, and who is not capable of assuming any greater responsibilities.

5. IMPROVEMENT IS NEEDED FOR CONTINUATION IN THE POSITION — This rating reflects less than satisfactory performance from employees who have had training and experience to perform the job, but who cannot handle the job requirements in an acceptable manner. Such employees will not be retained on the job for a prolonged period.

6. NEWLY APPOINTED TO POSITION — This rating is applicable to employees who have only recently assumed their current position.

PART V — ANALYSIS OF PERFORMANCE

A. What are his primary needs to improve his immediate performance?

_____
_____
_____
_____
_____

B. How can he acquire these capabilities? (Where and how can he learn what he needs to know to improve his management, technical or professional capabilities)? _____

_____
_____
_____
_____
_____

C. How have I, as his superior, assisted him to improve his performance? _____

_____
_____
_____
_____
_____

PART VI – POTENTIAL CATEGORIES

Check One:

_____ HIGH POTENTIAL – Employees who have *Exceptional Ability/Will to Excel.* Could rise to top positions in The Macke Company. Their potential is limited only by their personal motivation and/or the growth opportunities which the company provides.

_____ POTENTIAL – Employees who have the desire and apparent ability to progress beyond their current level. However, their progression is limited to one or two levels beyond their current position by age, education, or innate ability.

_____ STANDARD – Employees who make up the backbone of our workforce. They are dependable, reliable, and satisfactorily handle their current assignment but do not evidence potential for progression to higher level jobs.

_____ MARGINAL – Employees who are willing workers but are handling their current assignments in a marginal manner. They generally have been "standard" employees in the past but because of obsolescence, lack of motivation, or reorganization of the function, their performance is inadequate. (They will be informed of the necessary steps to improve by an established date.)

_____ SUB-MARGINAL – Employees who are lacking in both the desire and ability to satisfactorily perform their present assignment. Their potential to perform other assignments in an adequate manner is questionable. Their retention should be predicated on the company's ability to motivate then and find an appropriate assignment in which they can perform.

PART VII – EVALUATION OF POTENTIAL

A. Is he properly placed to realize his best potential for the company and for himself? What are his career goals?_____

_____

_____

_____

_____

B. What is the next step, if any, for this individual? (Identify position(s) for which he is qualified or will be qualified in the next year.)_____

_____

_____

_____

_____

184

C. What preparation does he require to successfully achieve this upward move? _____

_____

_____

D. Whom have you selected as this employee's back-up replacement to be ready to fill the promoted employee's position?_____

_____

_____

_____

PART VIII — DEVELOPMENT PLAN

Indicate specific action to be taken by you, the individual himself, or other management in meeting the individual's immediate and long-range needs. _____

_____

_____

_____

_____ _____
Signature of Employee   Date

_____ _____
Signature of Rater   Date

_____ _____
Signature of Rater's Supervisor   Date

_____ _____
Signature of Industrial Relations   Date
    Department Representative

Employee Evaluation Report — Non-Exempt

THE MACKE COMPANY
Non-Exempt Employee Evaluation

NAME: _____ COMPANY #: _____ BRANCH #: _____

POSITION: _____ REPORTS TO: _____

LENGTH OF SERVICE
IN POSITION RATED: _____

TOTAL YEARS
OF SERVICE: _____

PRESENT   EFFECTIVE   DATE OF
HOURLY RATE _____ DATE _____ THIS RATING: _____

INSTRUCTIONS TO RATER

An important responsibility of each level of supervision is an objective appraisal of the performance and potential of all personnel under his supervision. The purpose of this form is to provide answers to the following questions:

   A. How effective is the individual carrying out his presently assigned duties?
   B. What potential does he display for work in other fields or for the same fields at higher levels?
   C. What assistance, training or experience can we provide in order to:
      1. Increase his effectiveness or satisfaction with his present assignment?
      2. Develop his potential for the jobs to which he may be promoted or transferred?

I. *General*
   A. Base your "appraisal of current performance" on your observation of the individual's actual performance, not potential possibilities or hearsay.
   B. The rating should be for performance over the entire period covered by the review, not just most recent performance.
   C. Keep in mind the specific requirements of the job when considering each factor.

II. *Procedure*
   A. *Appraisal of Current Performance* — Part I. Consider each factor separately- and note in space provided any remarks that you feel best describe the individual and your reasons. Do not let your rating of an individual on one factor influence your rating on any other factor. It is unusual for an individual to be rated on all factors high or low. If you evaluate the employee carefully, you should reflect both high and low points.
   B. *Analysis of Performance* — Part II. Be sure to answer all questions. Please attach additional information if you feel it is helpful.

C. *Evaluation of Potential* — Part III. Fill out all questions based on your observations of the employee's general abilities. Please attach additional information or comments if you feel they are helpful.

D. *Directions for Completion* — Upon completion of Sections I, II, and III of this form:

1. Review the total appraisal form with your immediate superior and reconcile any questions necessary.

2. Go over the evaluation with the subject employee pointing out strong as well as weak points. Make definite suggestions for improving in areas you have shown to be weak or lacking.

3. Be sure that you have and allow sufficient interruption-free time to devote to the full evaluation.

E. *Distribution* — After interview is completed, forward this form to the Personnel Department. When a Personnel Action Notice is required, attach to the evaluation and send to the Personnel Department for final review.

REASON FOR REVIEW:

____ End of probation period (3 Months)
____ End of 6 months
____ End of 12 months
____ Semi-annual review
____ Merit
____ Transfer and/or promotion (Cross out one)

EVALUATION CODE: Mark employee's position on scale with a check (√).

E — (Exceptional) — Consistent performance of an outstanding nature.

AA — (Above Average) — Exceeds the satisfactory performance. Goes beyond the minimum requirement.

S — (Satisfactory) — Meets the minimum requirements.

NEA — (Not Entirely Acceptable) — Below expectations. Not completely acceptable, but may be able to overcome deficiencies.

U — (Unsatisfactory) — Has not yet met the requirements of the job. Potentially may never meet the standards expected.

PART I — APPRAISAL OF CURRENT PERFORMANCE

Knowledge of Job: Has a clear understanding of job and objectives.

E   AA   S   NEA   U

Comments: _____

_____

_____

Dependability: Conscientious, thorough in work assignments, accurate, on time to work, attendance, lunch, breaks, etc.

E   AA   S   NEA   U

Comments: _____

_____

_____

Judgment: Able to arrive at sound conclusions and make intelligent job decisions.

E   AA   S   NEA   U

Comments: _____

_____

_____

Initiative: Willing to accept increased responsibility, self-starting, independent.

E   AA   S   NEA   U

Comments: _____

_____

_____

Cooperation: Demonstrates ability and aptitude to work well with associates and subordinates. Is employee too sociable?

E   AA   S   NEA   U

Comments: _____

_____

_____

Quality of Work: Thoroughness, neatness and accuracy of all of work.

E   AA   S   NEA   U

Comments: _____

_____

_____

Quantity of Work: Volume of work acceptable under normal working conditions.

E   AA   S   NEA   U

Comments: _____

_____

_____

Adaptability: Employee ability to take sudden changes in procedures and work loads without losing efficiency and effectiveness.

E   AA   S   NEA   U

Comments: _____

_____

_____

Attitude: Job interest, Company interest, enthusiasm, passive resistance, constructive or destructive to team spirit.

E   AA   S   NEA   U

Comments: _____

_____

_____

PART II – ANALYSIS OF PERFORMANCE

1. What are employee's greatest strengths? _____

_____

_____

_____

2. What are employee's greatest weaknesses? _____

_____

_____

_____

3. Recommend definite actions to assist in improving employee's performance. _____

_____

_____

4. Is employee suited for present job? ___ Yes ___ No
   What is your recommendation? _____

_____

_____

_____

PART III – EVALUATION OF POTENTIAL

1. What, in your opinion, is employee's potential for additional growth? _____

_____

_____

_____

_____

   a. What area of responsibility (or specific job)? _____

_____

   b. Do you feel he can assume additional responsibility? _____

_____

c. If no, why not? _____

_____

_____

d. What do you recommend to prepare him for advancement?
   Experience: _____

_____

   Education or training: _____

_____

   Personnel development: _____

_____

   Other: _____

_____

PART IV — APPRAISAL INTERVIEW

1. Performance emphasizing the position requirements should be discussed frankly and objectively to:

   a. Point out areas of good performance
   b. Point out areas of weakness
   c. Let employee know where he stands
   d. Explain how employee may improve himself

2. In your discussion get information necessary to answer the following questions:

   a. Does employee have a specific goal?
   b. What does he believe is his strongest ability?
   c. What type of help does he want from you or the Company?
   d. What is he doing to help himself?
   e. What is employee's reaction?

   Employee's Comments: _____

_____

_____

_____

_____

_____

_____

Signature of Employee: Please sign as to your reading this complete evaluation.	Date
Signature of Reviewer	Date
Signature of Immediate Supervisor	Date
Signature of Authorized Personnel Representative	Date

ABOUT THE AUTHOR

FLOYD D. HEDRICK is Vice President for Purchasing for The Macke Company, one of the nation's largest vending and food service firms with headquarters at Washington, D.C. Prior to joining Macke, Mr. Hedrick was Purchasing Agent and Superintendent of Stores for Trailways Bus System.

He is a past president of the Purchasing Management Association of Washington, D.C. and is currently the chairman of the Food Industry Buyers Group of the National Association of Purchasing Management.

Active in AMA activities for several years, he has served as chairman of many seminars and workshops dealing with purchasing. Mr. Hedrick is presently a member of AMA's Purchasing Planning Council and is listed in a regional *Who's Who in America*. He is the author of several articles on purchasing that have appeared in trade publications and in AMA's *Management Review*.

Other publications
from the AMA Management Bookshelf

Purchasing and EDP
By A. E. Kollios and Joseph Stempel

Urges purchasing men to learn more about EDP and offers some basic information on how to get started with systems design, select hardware, and maintain purchasing control over an EDP procurement system. The authors describe in case-study fashion an actual automated procurement system at the Navy Aviation Supply Office.

$6.00/AMA members: $4.50

The Functions of the Purchasing Manager
By Manfredo Manente

An original schemata of the management process and its specific applications to the purchasing function. Divides the purchasing manager's functions into three broad categories: establishing objectives, actuating, and controlling.

$3.00/AMA members: $2.25

Systems Contracting
By Ralph A. Bolton

Describes a new purchasing concept and method designed to improve the reordering of repetitive-use materials with a minimum of expense. The author discusses the traditional purchase-order method of procurement, compares it with systems contracting, and shows in detail how to set up a working program of systems contracts.

$7.50/AMA members: $5.75

American Management Association, Inc.
135 West 50th Street   New York, N.Y. 10020

Cover design by Stuart Silver   0-8144-2147-4